# ANGEL INSIGHTS FOR UNPRECEDENTED TIMES

## ANGELS RAPHAEL AND ARIEL

### ADRIA WIND HORSE ESTRIBOU

Angel Insights for Unprecedented Times

Angels Raphael and Ariel

Channeled through Adria Wind Horse Estribou

First Edition (2020). Published in the United States.

Copyright © 2020 by Adria Estribou. All rights reserved. No part of this book may be used or reproduced in any manner whatsoever without written permission, except in the case of brief excerpts in critical reviews or articles.

Published by Wing Sound Media

www.WingSound.com

P.O. Box 3674

Sedona, AZ 86340

info@wingsoundmedia.com

Paperback
ISBN: 978-0-9971211-5-5

# CONTENTS

*Preface*     ix

### Part I
### FREEDOM

1. You are Free     3
2. The Sea Change     8
3. Upheaval Change     10
4. Instant Reality     13
5. The Bewilderment of Sudden Freedom     17
6. The Time of Choosing     23
7. Stepping into Every Choice     25

### Part II
### GREATER LIGHT

8. Rebalancing of Light     29
9. A Shift Toward Greater Light     32
10. Violence and Despair     36
11. You are the Light You Seek     40

### Part III
### WISHING & RECEIVING

12. It's Time to Receive     45
13. Creating Your World     49
14. Dropping Money as An Intermediary     52
15. How Can I Afford What I Wish For?     56
16. Creating from the Heart Center     58
17. Creating Negative—Oops!     64
18. Wishing for Health     67
19. What Should I Wish For?     70
20. Receiving QA     74

Part IV
## BECOMING
21. You are in the Field of God — 81
22. A Time of Becoming — 82
23. The Light Comes from You — 87
24. Finding Light Within Yourself — 90
25. You Are God — 92
26. The Bliss of the All — 95

Part V
## EMBODIMENT OF CHANGE
27. The Choice Between Third and Fifth Dimensions — 99
28. Physical Adaptations — 111
29. Ascending in the Physical Body — 116
30. Shedding Heavy Layers — 121
31. Telepathy — 130
32. You are Opening Doorways — 133
33. Sitting at the Round Table — 135
34. Sovereignty — 138

Part VI
## THE END OF CONTRACTS AND DESTINY
35. The End of a Lifetime — 145
36. Renegotiating & Daydreaming — 153
37. Dissolving Contracts — 155
38. Children — 159
39. Guilt & Joy — 163
40. Dropping Ancestral Lineages — 167
41. Wealth — 169
42. Work — 171
43. Soulmates — 173

Part VII
## ENLIGHTENMENT
44. What is Ascension? — 179
45. You are the Tapestry, Not a Thread — 181
46. The Void — 187
47. Dimensional Shifts Versus Enlightenment — 192

| | |
|---|---|
| 48. Enlightenment Pathways | 193 |
| 49. Receive Your Enlightenment | 198 |

Part VIII
WHAT ARE ANGELS?

| | |
|---|---|
| 50. The Primary Functions of Angels | 205 |
| 51. Not Above | 208 |
| 52. Your Angels | 209 |
| 53. Angels are Learning | 211 |
| 54. Humans and Angels | 213 |
| 55. Animals and Angels | 215 |
| 56. Angels and Reincarnation | 216 |
| 57. Call Upon Your Angels | 217 |
| 58. Seeing Angels | 220 |
| 59. Angel Numbers | 223 |

Part IX
WHAT'S NEXT?

| | |
|---|---|
| 60. Great Change on Cellular and Dimensional Levels | 229 |
| 61. Change Your World | 233 |
| 62. The Value of Time | 235 |
| 63. The Ease of Fifth Dimension | 242 |
| Closing Prayer | 246 |
| *About the Author* | 249 |

"Please know that we are with you at all times. You may call on us at any time for any reason. We are ready to serve with you, dance with you, and be in all kinds of light with you. We do not shy away from any of these types of experiences you will face. Whether you see them as positive or negative, we are neutral to facing them, understanding them, enjoying them with you."

- Angel Raphael

# PREFACE

What an extraordinary, bewildering, intense, and awe-inspiring time to be alive!

After 30 years of meditating and an active spiritual journey, I had reached a sense of steadiness, calm and happiness that more or less defined my experience of daily life. The energetic changes on Earth have rocked every part of my world—my identity, sense of how the world works, and my emotional, physical, and spiritual experiences.

In September 2018, I had a palpable feeling we had "arrived" somewhere new. Although things looked the same externally, energetically they felt extraordinarily different. For me there were some initial weeks of waves of bliss and euphoria.

Since then, the unfolding of these new energies—and myself along with them—have felt like a wild and unpredictable ride in the unknown. This time defies all my concepts of what I thought ascension was going to feel like. Along with heightened states of unity consciousness, stretches of "no mind," expansion and lightness of being, have come intensely uncomfortable physical symptoms, emotional clearing, and the frustration (and sometimes outright

PREFACE

panic) of trying to function "normally" amidst such high fluctuating energies and clearings.

At first I thought this was something dramatic in my personal journey, but then something very interesting started to happen. In sharp contrast to my channeling work in 2017, in 2018 I started to see that big themes were coming up again and again for multiple people and in group sessions. These are what I'd call "universal" from the standpoint of people undergoing the energetic transitions on the planet now that began in approximately January 2018.

Angels Raphael and Ariel spoke through me about these collective changes. They answered the big questions I had: "This feels huge, but what exactly is going on here?" And: "Where is the operating manual for this New Earth? How do things work here?"

It is my understanding that the themes gathered in this book (channeled in 2018 and 2019 in Hawaii) will continue to be resonant for us for at least the next few years as we shift and evolve into the brilliant new energetic times we're in. Because although the new energies became somewhat instantly available to all of us, it is a transition time for us physically to adapt and also to change our belief patterns so we don't keep recreating things in the old ways we're accustomed to understanding the world.

It also appears that a group of us are exploring these energies more actively first in order to mentor those just a step or two behind us through this transition. Because it's new for all of us, more than ever it's time for us to share with those around us what we're learning about this new world. On a quantum level (like the 100th monkey), whatever steps we take on this journey do show the way for others, even when they occur on our meditation cushions at home where no one else seems to be watching. This is a shared journey.

I am so grateful to be with you in such profound and unprecedented times.

It is my wish that the messages in this book help you better understand the beautiful paradox of these shifting times, how to navigate our new freedoms, and that the angels' words are there for you when you fall occasionally into despair or doubt and need to be reminded how bright your light is and how unlimited the world is for you now. (Yes, right now!)

With love,

*Adria*

P.S. As this book goes to press, fears of a global pandemic are permeating the media and daily life. Now, more than ever, it feels important for us to know what the angels have to teach us about our freedom, our right to create the life we want, and our ability to do so without anything more powerful or complicated than our sovereign will.

# PART I
# FREEDOM

## THE SEA CHANGE

# YOU ARE FREE

## ANGEL ARIEL

It is as if the prison doors have been flung open now. Humanity is now free from what has been different types of enslavement through most of humanity's history. You might not have visibly seen shackles on your arms, but you were chained to—let us say for shorthand—prescribed ways of being, certain pathways which were allowed and many which were not allowed. And now you are in this wide, wide, open time, when everything is open. You are quite free.

What happens in any kind of change, the human system first feels a little nervous. "I don't know if I want to walk through that doorway. Even though the angel is telling me that is freedom. I've always lived over here. And my grandfather lived over here and my mother and my sister and we all only know what's going on in here. So why would I go over there?"

There is this very natural timidity when change arises. You have seen that in your children, you've seen that in yourself. It is a beautiful human response. It doesn't need to be judged, but just see it for what it is. The sort of discomfort right now is not because we are in a dark time. In fact, we are in quite a light time. But it feels a little unhinged.

The door is literally off its hinge. So you might feel uncertain what to do with all of this freedom.

Now is the time to receive what you wish for. Before, you can relate now to this metaphor, when you were a child it was the teacher or the parent or society telling you: "This is what it's time to do now." As you grew up, you thought both angels and guides, I should ask them: "What is it time to do now?" Because I want to be a good student, a good human, I want to help others . . . There might be different reasons for asking the question.

But still, we are used to being told what do, yes? So we come to the angels and say: "Okay, what do I do now?" And now your angels and guides are saying: "What do you want to do?" Not in a flippant way. But really, what do you want to do? Because now it's open. You can truly create the world that you desire. We phrased it as receiving because it used to be more of an uphill struggle.

There were always, always exceptions to the rule. There were always those who knew how to go off road even though a certain pathway was prescribed. There were always those throughout humanity's history who succeeded in receiving what they want. Or we would use the word "creating" or "manifesting," something that seems a little harder to do. So there were always those who knew how to forge those pathways for themselves. But as a whole, humanity has been in this sheep-like stage, where [due to] constraints that were beyond their control, in many instances, they were being herded towards one thing or another.

So you have this deep, deep habit—it goes back through your ancestral roots, and many generations, to the beginning of humankind—of being told what to do. And so here you come with these good intentions: "Please tell me what to do, because this whole wide-open world, I don't know, it seems a little frightening." And you receive back maybe no answer, or things just don't seem as clear. You used to feel like your path was so clear, and now it feels uncertain.

We want you to know, it is not because the world is suddenly a place that's uncomfortable to inhabit. It's because you have not yet decided where you want to go. It's not because the pause button is from the outside from the universe saying: "Hold on, you can't have that yet." It's because you haven't quite trusted yourself yet, because this is so new, to know in fact you can have exactly what you want. And you can have it now. The old way, when you were 10 years old or two years ago was: "Okay, you can wish for that. You can make a vision board, you can have a goal and maybe 40 years from now you can have that."

The new way is just be very clear about what you want, and have it now.

The only caveat we add here is if you are intending to harm another, it won't work. Those energies are not so supported. If you intend to harm another, it's a little more like the old way where maybe you can still do it, but it's going to be much harder. So you see there is still violence on the planet around, there are some vestiges of that. But there has been such a change toward freedom, you are going to see less and less of that. And those that are still attracted to violence, to harming one another, are going to make little pods and reinforce for each other: this is how the world is. While the rest of us will be dancing free, and celebrating the fact that there is so much less violence on the planet. So it's not that it disappears entirely. But it does not need to rule your existence the way it used to. You are no longer under that iron fist, that thumbprint of someone or something else telling you: "This is what you must do. This is how you must behave."

So how do you manage this complete chaos? You step out into a world where you don't know the rules, and you don't know how it works. That is where the guidance comes in. Because you still have these angels and friends around whether they're embodied friends who are very sensitive, or teachers that you look towards, or family members. You still have wise ones around you whether they are embodied or not embodied. But they're looking to you to direct the questions a little more now. So instead of asking: "What should I do now?" Maybe you could ask: "How do I really explore what my gifts are? What are really my options, given this physical body in this time period on the planet and how the dimensional realities are mixing? What's open to me today?"

Start to think in terms of options and in terms of what you want in the core of you. And then you will see your world organizes itself around that. It is no longer you organizing yourself around the world, but the world organizing itself around you. You'll see we will each be creating very different worlds. So in this time, when it is a little more of the chaos of freedom of newness, you might be having very, very distinctly different experiences than those around you. Some people around you still believe nothing has changed because they haven't experienced otherwise other than maybe feeling like they have the flu and things seem a little strange. And their mind is so strong. The mind is habitual, yes? So it knows to tell you how things have always worked in the past.

The mind is very good at remembering and recreating history, because it knows how to remember and repeat, remember and repeat. So that's one option. Even though you have this freedom, you can stay in the prison cell. If it's more comfortable for you, and we say this without judgment, you can continue to create the same kind of world that you grew up in. You, as a free being, completely have that right and your angels and your guides and the universe around you will reorganize the world to keep it looking "sameness" around you. Because if that feels more comfortable, if it feels more loving to you, you can have that. You do not have to jump into this wildly new experience. For those of you who are adventure seekers or just ready because, "Come on after all these generations it's time, I want the freedom!" bust out and experience, experiment ...

The other thing is the moment you walk through this door, you're not being asked to choose between 40 paths and then you're stuck with that the rest of your lifetime and those coming after you, their lifetimes. No, you can experiment a little. It is more like you walk through this doorway and it is an open field. There are no paths. So where do you want to walk? What's attractive to you? Is it the trees over here or the lake over here? Would you like to just sit down and look inward? For those of you who have been very curious about galactic beings, planetary travel, that becomes much, much more available. But again, some beings are going to feel very threatened and frightened by such an idea. So they will ask [to] be shielded, their vision, from that kind of experience. It is like this, where truly you create your world.

# THE SEA CHANGE

## ANGEL RAPHAEL

*Q: Is there a coming ascension event?*

FROM OUR PERSPECTIVE, this event has happened already. Very approximately in January 2018 there was such a shift for humankind, such freedom where before there was bondage, that what you are in now is the time of exploring that, of learning what it is, of coming into owning—in the sense of feeling comfortable in the skin of your new freedom.

It's already yours. There are more openings, more portals, more windows in an astrological sense, and there will be more beings coming to the planet to help. So yes, there will be more events, there will be more shifts in consciousness. But the large event from our perspective, this sea change, has already occurred. And it is in large part why so many people feel so lost right now. It's not because we are in the dark before the light, it's because it is completely unfamiliar to humankind, generally speaking, to be so free.

This is the time now of adjusting to, adapting to, the freedom, which is a much easier road. It's a more confusing road, because that linear sense of battle, of purpose, was easy to follow. Now, when the battle has been won, when the freedom has been gained, it's a little confusing to those who are looking for that singular purpose that they have followed over multiple lifetimes to come into freedom, where you are truly making the choices and not choosing between lesser evils, so to speak, where everything is wide open to joy, to growth, to any kind of experience you want to have here now.

That is quite confusing to a soul that has been so limited, in the sense the walls have been so close around you defining what is possible for generations. And now when there are no walls, it's very, very confusing. But that doesn't mean it's a dark time or a difficult time. From our perspective, it just means quite naturally you are in chaos and confusion.

Let's stay with this metaphor of walls which were there, which now are no longer there. If out of fear, people are going to turn to the rubble and try to hold on to a few of those rocks, that's all right. It's a natural response. But it doesn't mean they're going to erect that same tall wall. So you don't need to be in fear of going backwards. Humanity collectively is not going to go backwards because of this fear response. But it does get less and less over time—the fear—as people test out the new boundaries or lack of boundaries and see what this new way of being feels like. Then the fear becomes less and less as the demonstration is there of: What is this time? How is it different?

Conceptually, we understand how it's confusing for those who have been expecting an event that looks like blinding light and the angels visible before them and a scroll that says: "Here's how it works now" and "step this way." It doesn't look like that. It doesn't fit that old concept. But it's much, much better than that, let's say it that way. We are usually quite neutral. But we must be on the side of believing this is a better reality for humanity, because it is so evidently so.

# UPHEAVAL CHANGE

## ANGELS RAPHAEL, URIEL AND GABRIEL

We bring you a message of peace in troubling times. The human spirit seeks balance and equanimity. So when there are times of strife or unevenness in our experience, we feel unsettled. Humans feel unsettled with conditions that are rocky and uncertain and in upheaval. Angels admire above all on this planet Earth the ability for humans to eject out from themselves past experience; to learn and grow from the new; in a sort of volcanic way to erupt outward energetically; to slough off what is no longer needed on the soul level.

This is a very dynamic plane of existence. This type of upheaval change is not available in other planes. It is a blessing from our perspective. It is a blessing to live in a time of upheaval and change, because in it there are so many multitudes of ways that you can release what no longer serves your highest understanding, your highest belief, and to move forward in your own lifetime. You don't need to carry around the shells of past understanding because of the upheaval energy available.

There is this beautiful spark within you that resonates with the ability to let go in a sort of forceful way, in a sort of eruptive way. This is what you are seeing reflected around you—this energy of revolt, rebellion, upheaval, is very, very akin to those volcanic energies of the earth.

What happens when the volcano erupts, explodes all of that light and pent up anxieties and pressures? What happens other than relief that it is done, is that new land has formed. New landscapes. New types of plants are nurtured in a different new soil.

What you face now is very much like that. You can view it as catastrophic change, the way a volcano forms earth is quite catastrophic if viewed from a certain way. Or, you can view it as the miraculous ability for new earth to be formed, where what had been there before was so stale and set in its ways. You can view it either way. The choice is up to you. What you cannot choose, while on this Earth plane at this moment in her history, is to live in a time that does not carry the energy of upheaval. What you can choose is how to use that energy in your own soul for your growth, and for forming new vistas, new landscapes for your playfields in the future.

The choice is up to you. Change will happen whether or not you are on board with the fact that change will happen. This very earth changes in each moment. Your very body system changes in each moment. The cells are not the same as they were yesterday, or one hour ago, or what they will be an hour hence.

The choice of how you view this volcanic time is up to you. Is it a treasure—the miracle of birth? Or is it the erupting disruption of all that you have known before? Both are the same, truly. And you cannot put a volcano back inside of itself the way you can put a cork on a bottle. You cannot stop the momentum of energies of change on this plane of existence right now. Nor can you stop your own soul's evolution. But how you choose to witness these events—these changes—that is entirely up to you.

*Angel Ariel:*

In the time of unraveling of the old ways, it is predictable chaos. Meaning, you could have foreseen, any of us could have foreseen coming into this juncture of great change, that there would be fear and upheaval.

But from our point of view, it is such a beautiful, beautiful upheaval. To use the metaphor of a prison, if humanity were inside and some beneficial beings, angels among them, were ripping down the walls of the outer prison . . . it's quite noisy, and there's debris falling, and it seems quite chaotic. But isn't it lovely that you're free?

# INSTANT REALITY

## ANGEL ARIEL

*W*hat is happening for humankind right now, generally? What is available to humankind? The same way that ozone pollution or global warming might be available to everyone at the same moment but people deal with it in different ways, there are energy patterns and changes in human consciousness which are available generally. And then here's where the free will comes in, that you get to choose: "Do I really want this? Or do I want to have the minimum of this—to go in an ozone-free bunker and not experience the change?"

You have those options: all the way from transcendence to staying where you are now. You have all those options. But we'll speak about what generally is available now to humankind. And it's new. So we speak a lot about this in these days, in these next few months, because if you get on a ship and move to Greenland, you're quite aware that you moved somewhere, and there's probably different currency and you need to learn some things. But if the change happens while you're still in your same house, in your same job with your same family, maybe you don't notice that something very large has changed. So that's the news that we bring is what this change is.

"Instant reality" has to do with how much you are now in charge of what you want in your life. Always there has been a role for the human heart, the human mind, to choose what direction to go in life. But very generally speaking, it used to be a much harder road. When you were a child, even two years ago, when you set about doing something, finding someone to date, or a certain kind of job, or certain kind of healing gift you wanted to give to the world ... Maybe it was at least a six-month course of study, or a lot of intentionality and some different rituals around bringing that into being. You knew it was possible, but it took a long time. And in some cases, perhaps money was another ingredient there. So what happens now it's as if money and time were pulled out of the equation. What is left—if money and time were between what you wanted, and having it right now—then you move into having it right now.

It's a little bit to get used to. The first few times that it happens, perhaps you think it is synchronicity, coincidence. "Oh, I _just_ wished for that. Well, that must have been coming along and I felt it was coming along, so I just happened to be on the same bus and there was the ad on bus for the job I just wished for." Some of it is about keeping your eyes open now and not expecting that it's going to take so long for your wish to come true. Of course, you might have some role in that—picking up the phone and calling the number on the ad of what is so clearly your job that just appeared.

So maybe it doesn't always arrive on your doorstep, wrapped in a bow. But we say that in general for humankind with time and money taken out as necessary ingredients to get what you want, now you really can have what you want.

The caveat we add here: if what you want is to harm other people, that actually is becoming more difficult. So the good news for the rest of us is that reality becomes more and more difficult to force—still possible, still humanly possible on this planet at this time, but it becomes less and less. Instead, what we are moving into is a time where like children, in the most beautiful sense, we get to have what we want. And not like bratty children or stealing from another to have it. But like children who in their innocence have not been talked out of the fact they can have whatever they want, whenever they want it. We do ask please play with this and let your wishes be either big or small. But don't discount just because last year you wished for that thing and it didn't come true, that doesn't mean that now, today, it won't come true so instantly. We want you to be aware, although it wasn't so obvious to most of you—you didn't move to another country—and yet the rules of operation of where you are still living are that different. It takes some adjusting to learn new ways. And the good news is they are much easier ways.

It is not as in the past when you had to move through such different difficult astrological times or more violent times, and so forth. Now, just short term, and we don't mean three to five days, but let's say three to five years or so give or take, it is a little rocky on the planet. It's so new and a little jarring sometimes when the energy changes that much. So for that reason, it might feel a little bit chaotic or, like occasionally the ground slips under your feet. It does feel a little rocky to some who are sensitive right now energetically, but it is not because it's a difficult time. It's just because change is so rapid, and part of the rapid change is—here's the beauty of free will here in the collective—part of the rapid change is a quickening, let's say. Because so many of you are wishing for enlightenment and for good things for the planet as a whole, that amplifies the change that's happening and it's happening even more quickly than it would have naturally.

It is a beautiful time of opening to: what are the wishes in your soul? What are your wishes for humanity? Your wishes do not have to be just for you. But understand that because you are surrounded by other free-will beings, those who wish to have a different experience than you will probably go off in a different part, energetically or physically speaking, a different part of the island or different workplaces so that they can be around people who want what they want. It's just a natural thing. That happens now—you go somewhere where you like the music and other people are there who like that same music.

Similarly, as you wish for certain energetic realities you find: "Isn't it curious that suddenly there are so many people around me who want the same kind of energies. Where before it was so hard to meet people like that." Well, now there's this beautiful amplification as others wish for similar types of healing gifts or energies, suddenly you meet each other, you find each other in the same areas—sometimes physically, sometimes through webinars or other types of space. So space need not be an obstacle here, either, although that's not so much the shift we're talking about tonight.

So what is instant reality? Is it like instant oatmeal? And is it less nourishing then, and we should avoid it? Or is it just that things got so fast, and so we better slow down, like slow food? There's a lot of concepts in your current reality that would tell you that "instant reality" is probably not a good idea. So let's speak about that a little bit. What are the doubts here? Why would you want something to take a long time to mature—like a tree taking several years to grow and then the fruit maturing on that tree?

Well, if you really wanted to learn that fruit comes from a tree, couldn't you learn that just by walking down the street and picking a fruit from a tree that already spent all its years growing? We think you can. We don't think the lessons necessarily have to be so slow. So we are being a little frivolous here in our example, but from angelic perspective, we want you to know that just because things can happen very fast here, it does not mean that what you are wishing for and what you receive should be discounted just because it came so fast. It doesn't mean it comes from a negative source or a lesser source. The speed of light is very fast. The speed of angels, the speed of human thought is very fast. The world now is opening up to move as quickly as your heart wants it to. And some of you will want a slower pace and that is what you will wish for and that is what you will receive. It is very compassionate that way. But just because it is so fast does not mean it is something to be feared.

# THE BEWILDERMENT OF SUDDEN FREEDOM

## ANGEL RAPHAEL

You might be feeling a little confused about how to operate in the new now. Things have shifted quite a lot and many of you have felt this letting go of a lot of the ties to the third-dimensional [ways], we would say the practical day-to-day reality of living on the planet. So that leaves you perhaps feeling somewhat adrift. A little bit lost, perhaps, if you're looking to find your footing in the same old ways. The same old ways meaning: operating in a linear sense, looking for a logical path for the mind and the heart to follow. If you were still trying to force through in that old linear three-dimensional way you might feel disgruntled at this point, or confused, or bewildered.

There is a reason for that. There is a new operational system you might say, in computer terminology, here on the planet, and things don't work quite the way they used to. Really not at all the way they used to. And yet we still have jobs, some of us. There are still bills to pay. There are still telephones and cars on the road. So things in a sense look very much the same. And yet they are not.

So what do we do in this new now? How do we take hold of what is coming forward?

The biggest lesson in this we can share is not to try so hard through the old ways. If something seems familiar to the mind and it is not working anymore, it's because that link to the old three-dimensional reality is broken.

You have intentionally asked to be uplifted as the Earth uplifts, as humanity uplifts at this time. And so you have. You have been part of this transition. Some people—many people—have chosen to stay in the very practical third-dimensional reality. That is a choice that is open to all here on the planet also. So you might be confused why some of your friends seem to be going along even busier at work, those same old three-dimensional ways are working even better for them. Yet for you, you feel perhaps a bit lost—out of touch with how to move forward in the new now.

One thing that is being asked of you right now is to listen. To simply listen to what is around you—and we do not necessarily mean with the physical ears. For some of you that will be the case. You can listen with your eyes also. Or with your heart. What is it you are being called to now?

Perhaps your old purposes, your ways of being, are done. Perhaps it is not possible to move through these same three-dimensional circuitry methods any longer. If that is the case, what are you being called to now? If you have been freed from the old structures, what does your heart want? What do your eyes see that looks delightful (not tempting, but delightful)? What do your ears hear that feels like music? Whether it is the leaves moving in the trees, the waterfall, the actual music . . . What is it that is making your heart dance? It might be quite different than what it was last year. And you might be causing yourself some unnecessary heart pains by trying to make it the same as it was last year.

You have on the whole been freed from large constructs, let us say, that were holding you into, embracing you into a type of prison-like reality in the third dimension. Now that you are free from that, it is also a little bit like trying to drive still but there are no longer any roads or traffic signals or rules of the road. So yes the tremendous freedom is there, but also—for a short time perhaps—confusion is also there. "Well I knew what to do when there was a road and stoplight, and now am quite unsure."

Please know that you are not being asked to make this transition suddenly. You are not being asked to suddenly understand how to navigate fifth and higher dimensions. This will come.

It is a little bit like the day that someone gets out of prison. The shackles are removed from feet and hands. They are not asked that day when they are released from prison to take on some new mountainous task. They are asked to be free. To enjoy freedom. To rest. That is the period of time you are in.

If you're feeling this listlessness, floaty reality, it is fine to enjoy that, and not to feel that you need to force yourself back into a doership reality. Money will come. Opportunities will come. You are probably finding this is the case in quite surprising ways. It is not that you are being released from prison without means to feed yourself. No. The banquet is there. The place to rest is there.

The mind feels uneasy because it does not have the 'to do' list anymore. It doesn't know now that the structure—to continue with the prison metaphor—the very structured life of when to get up, when to work, is no longer there. So what do we do with ourselves? First we would say please enjoy the freedom. Understand it for what it is, which is a moment of freedom that will last. It is not temporary. And as you get your sea legs, so to speak, as you become more used to functioning in fifth and higher dimensional realities, you will understand what the choices are and what is asked of you moving forward.

This day (and we do not literally mean this day, but following the metaphor), this day that you are released from prison, nothing is asked of you. You are truly being invited to rest and enjoy the fact that you are out of prison. Following the metaphor again, you may have seen in literal prisons in this Earth third dimension, that people who come out of prison lifestyle are quite disoriented, sometimes for a while find it very difficult to enjoy this new freedom. So you can understand that you are not the first one to feel bewildered at being so free.

But it does help the mind to feel some comfort that what is happening here is a transition. Freedom. It is not that you have lost your way. You have lost your imprisonment, which is something you hoped to lose.

*Q: What is propelling this shift from imprisonment into freedom?*

Many, many light workers have worked through generations, and predicted this time bursting out into freedom on this planet. Many races also—galactic races—joined with humankind in this, in precipitating this moment of freedom. It was certainly not accidental. Many sages some hundreds of years ago, meditating in a cave, many people talking in front of crowds last year, many different ways of what we would call light work (to fit your vocabulary here) . . . so it was quite intentional. There was a pushing the boulder over the edge, and the moment arrived when freedom was quite inevitable and did occur. It was as a result of many of your lifetimes specifically working towards this.

You have arrived. And that is where some of the confusion comes, because you have been pushing towards this goal for so many lifetimes, and now here you are. The goal is achieved. So what the heck do you do with yourself? That is the moment that we find ourselves in. The strange bewilderment of having won the war, and no longer having a battle to fight.

Certainly there are still what we might call dark forces here and there in the universe, in the corners and sometimes quite violently in politics and those sorts of arenas, but largely we would say there is no longer a battle, nothing that needs to be won at this moment. For those of you who have been a warrior or priestess in so many lifetimes, now you come into this moment of great freedom, of great peace in this one, and it is bewildering. It is bewildering to come out into the plateau of this great peaceful horizon.

~

*Q: You said we are in a very peaceful time, but the media situation doesn't feel that way.*

How to reconcile what appears to be a more violent, a more backward time than in recent memory certainly? What to understand about what is happening in the very public media arenas specifically? Let us look at that.

There are two elements of this. One is that some people are holding onto third dimensional reality. They are making that choice to stay, and you will see that reflected more in the political arena and media arena specifically—movies, television and so forth. So if you do not resonate with what is happening there, you are free to change the channel, we would say. Meaning, it does not affect your life as much as perhaps it used to—in 1970 or some other time when it was important for everyone to rise up and make changes in a political sense. What you are seeing now is a little different. It is not that you need to be complacent with bigotry or anything else in your life, but understand that you have the choice to live in a very different world—a different structural system. And many people are choosing to stay in the third dimension right now.

Partially what is happening is you are seeing from some distance now the starkness of third dimension untempered by angelic and other forces. The other piece in this: It is a little bit like a kingdom that has been surrounded, in siege; it knows it is going to die soon. You could call this things like patriarchy if you like, that's not quite a word we would choose but just to give some sense here—bigotry certainly, the sense that any people or animals are smaller than I am. Any of those ways of thinking about the world. That consciousness has been encircled now in siege. There is no way for it to rule on this planet in a true sense. And yet it is making so much noise. And that is the noise of the dying soul, if you want to use that analogy. It is the noise of the last battle cry for those who have already lost.

So from our perspective—angelic perspective—it is not a call to sensitive conscious beings to change leadership politically. It is the call to step back from third-dimensional reality entirely. To understand that we have a choice as the path splits, which way, which direction to take. Even in your lifetime that was not the case; it was an important time for humankind to assert their consciousness in a political way. And that was part of your evolution. It was part of your conscious growth. Right now it is something else. Is not that people who assert their consciousness in a political way are wasting their energies. But we are in a very different landscape now. What is required for the Earth is humans upon it to lift up. Lifting up has already happened, so you can think of this as the screaming of the dying animal as it falls from the cliff. There is really not much you need to do to make that happen. It has already happened.

# THE TIME OF CHOOSING

## ANGEL RAPHAEL

This is still the time of choosing for many. They are waking up. Many have known about conscious undertakings for several lifetimes. So this is not new [for them]. For many on the planet, they are seeing these types of things for the very first time. So they will be choosing in these few years which direction to go with this, whether to uplift or to cling to third dimension, because it seems too scary to do otherwise. Even for those of you who are quite conscious it is still sometimes a little bit daunting to be in this very, very new plane of existence.

Quite generally we would say a few years' time when there is this sifting and choosing. It is not abrupt and immediate also to be compassionate to those in humankind who are perceiving their choices for the first time, so that they can digest this a little and make the choice. For that reason it is a little bit here and there and back again for these few years. Even though as we have said the battle has been won and you are quite free.

Even those who choose third dimension are quite free. That's why they are free to choose to stay in that dimensional reality. We would add from angelic perspective there is not so much judgment on that choice to stay with the third dimension. For those who choose to stay in third dimension it is not because they are necessarily so dense that they are not ready, or some sort of judgmental way of looking at it, but that they have specific lessons they would like to learn here that are easier to do in that system of third dimension.

It has to do with that also, on a soul level what lessons you came in to learn in this lifetime. Even though you are in the time of great change, perhaps not all the souls came in for that in this lifetime. And they would like to take advantage of this last period of third dimension to live out the lessons in that way.

## STEPPING INTO EVERY CHOICE

### ANGEL RAPHAEL

*A*s a child, you were given some choice, perhaps what color shirt to wear, or whether or not to eat dinner. So you had some choice there. But now as an adult, you have more choices, but still it has been within a confined structure that is somewhat choiceless at this point in your road. So it is difficult to see how you could suddenly step into every choice. But this is what we are moving into on a planetary level—the ability to choose from day to day and then change your mind and choose something else. So you will not be locked in any longer to the length of time it took to get a PhD in something and then work your way up a few jobs doing that, and then you get the right connections . . . It is more day-to-day this experimenting and play with what types of energies to relate to and where you want to take your energy and enthusiasm. We say this word "play" because it is like that. It is not so serious anymore, and it is not so hard anymore.

Really humankind—we will say generally without going into the whole history—has been in this prison structure on Earth since the beginning, almost the beginning. It is difficult for the human consciousness to understand that there is something other than prison. There is. And you are now free to explore it. It is just so new that it will take some time to acclimate.

Like being set down at the top of the mountain, your lungs do have the capacity to breathe that air. But it is new; it is different. It will take a little time. You might feel sluggish and tired for some time as you begin to understand that your thoughts become the world around you.

Masters have taught this for eons, but you will begin to see in your own lives how easy it is and how true that is: that what you create in your mind, in your heart, becomes your world. So, this idea of needing to exchange a certain amount of money and needing certain family connections, of needing to have been born a certain race, or at a certain point in history becomes unnecessary. Those are falsehoods. We each do have this access to full abundance that is as wide as your imagination will allow it to grow.

What we are working on collectively here in the next years is expanding our imagination to what is possible. Creating it, seeing it fulfilled. Some of you will be better at this, and they will be new leaders, in a sense, the new mentors to show others how easy it is. Then you can follow—like children in the best sense, just seeing something new, being awed by it, and trying it yourself.

We are certainly in a time of full abundance on this planet. It is not something that is coming in the future. It is here now. It is just rewiring the brain, or letting that part of the brain that doesn't believe that to be ignored, however it works for you. You already right in this moment have full access to every abundance.

# PART II
# GREATER LIGHT

# REBALANCING OF LIGHT

## ANGEL RAPHAEL

*E*ach of you here have felt currents of energies quite strongly in different ways at different times. Some of you from different places on the Earth's body, and some of you from animal communications, and some of you from starlight.

It is as if the human body is becoming more of a conductor for these energies. It is morphing into something much more conducive to conducting celestial light and other kinds of light. Whereas before it might be like light falling on an object and just illuminating it for the eye of something else to see, now the light enters the human body, and the human body is not a collector of the light, but a conductor of it.

Humans are entering a different time in their evolution, where instead of primarily learners they are also now becoming the fixers in a sense of the mistakes they have made, energetically becoming conduits to move and shape light and energy. And dance with it, yes, but more importantly, to help to redirect and heal not just the Earth, but ourselves, each other, the other species on this planet . . . helping to redress.

Humankind, in one way of viewing things, has done more harm than many other species in any of these layers of existence. And yet, it is because they have been manipulated to do so for the most part. So now free from that manipulation something in the soul, the human soul, wants to balance that. Even though you might say it was not our fault as humans, and this is true, still the beauty of the human heart and how it works, it wants to balance and find that balance like the Yin Yang. Understanding there was the violence and pain and unnecessary suffering, it now wants to flood the world and the Earth and the other humans and the butterflies with this love, beautiful qualities of light.

That is the time you are entering into now on this planet—on this plane of existence rather, for you will join with other planetary systems in this—it is a rebalancing of light. You have as a human species been acknowledging the dark aspects of light for some centuries now. And now it is just as if you have turned over onto the other side of the rotating planet onto the side that is light. And now the human bodies and souls wish to be vehicles for this light.

It is dancing with the same energy. It is all God's light. But you are now as humankind wanting to dance with the brighter, whiter aspects of that light. That is a more conceptual way, not a literal way of speaking of it. But certainly what in your perception is more delightful, more enjoyable, lighter, more balanced. So what comes on this plane of existence now—not limited to this planet but this plane of communication and existence—is a euphoria beyond what you have been able to experience in the past.

It is not so much about a ladder of evolution, as many human seers have been conceiving of this time in history. It is not so much about the learning ladder as it is balancing the dark light with the light light. Having had so much of the heaviness and suffering, it is now this outpouring of light. Filling in that light portion of the Yin Yang in that metaphor and sometimes in a literal sense. This is the time we are in, just on the cusp of, so you have begun to taste each of you these energies pouring through you at moments where it is nothing that the body or the mind thought it was doing, but suddenly you are caught up in this bliss or movement or shaking or wakefulness.

It is that you have begun to understand you are fibers in this new light, this new awakening light. It is quite a party, you might say. Quite an extraordinary time to be alive on this plane of existence. Especially for those who have experienced the polarity of suffering, you can appreciate the light. Like those who have come out of the dark of night can understand the daylight in a way that those who are on planes of existence and planets that only have the bright light cannot. You will celebrate even more than your brothers and sisters on other planets and planes of existence because you have tasted the darkness so sweetly.

You have been in that experience so long through so many generations in your ancestry and your own incarnations that coming into this light now is just the sweetest surprise. It is such a contrast. Whereas one lifetime from now those who are still choosing to embody as humans on this plane of existence may find it quite humdrum to be in so much light and movement and energy. It will become quite commonplace. But for you who have chosen to be embodied at this line or cusp of the Yin Yang, you understand, you can experience the extraordinary nature of the change of it.

Which is not to say that it will not cycle again back toward the dark light because things want to stay in balance. That is why we see it as a misperception that it is a ladder of evolution, from darkness into light. We see this all as God's light—the dark light and light light. But you have many, many celebrations of light for some generations to come on this planet because, very generally speaking, since the beginning of humankind it has been the dark light in this plane of existence. So now you have quite some time ahead of you of this light.

## A SHIFT TOWARD GREATER LIGHT

### ANGEL RAPHAEL

Some of you have been wondering where this greater lightening—that so many angels and guides have been speaking of—where it is? When will you personally begin to feel it? The energies of this eclipse have allowed a great opening within you personally. This is a more personal time for the light to shine through. And the groundwork that has been laid on a planetary level will now be more perceivable to you. Many who have been sensitive to planetary and environmental energies have felt this for some months already, and now those of you whose awareness is more contained in your own being begin to feel what these others have been speaking about.

What does it mean to enter a time of greatening light? Does it mean ease and harmony? It does not, not necessarily. Although within yourself you might taste the delicious nature of greatening light, and enjoy it more than the mixed sensations of light mixed with dark. That is up to your personal choice and preference. What we bring you now (by "we" we mean the collective cosmic forces bringing about this great change) is greatening light for yourself, for your personal being. Not that it is meant to be hoarded of course. But what we mean is now you can perceive it as individual. Of course in a true sense you are not separate and distinct from the environment and the cosmic forces, and the greatening light that has beheld your planet. But not all of you are sensitive enough to perceive this, and some of you have been experiencing it as a time of great fear.

So now we enter an era where it becomes easier on the individual level to perceive this light. So what is it about—this greatening light? Light and darkness are the dichotomies of your world. Although everything is of one Great Spirit, one great God-ness, you still perceive it in this dichotomy of light and dark, and we have this tendency to associate light with God. This is not the case. What we mean is light is no more God than dark is. But light could be expressed as a tendency of the soul to uplift towards its greatest purpose here, to uplift towards service to others, to uplift toward light. In its fundamental being-ness light is a quality, and a state of being, that cannot be described in words. And yet we wish to emphasize that it is not better than—it is not a state of goodness greater than—dark.

*[Note: From time to time the angels speak about astrological events and the energies they bring with them. Although this message was particularly about a full lunar eclipse on July 27, 2018, it resonates very strongly still because we are in a time when there is so much more light, and more can be seen.]*

That is why the eclipse is such a beautiful time to embrace your wholeness. A time when a light you are used to perceiving is covered in a beautiful blanket of dark. It may frighten you to hear an angel speak of darkness with so much love. We do not come from the same dichotomy of your world, so light and dark to us look like the many flavors of your universe. In the angelic realms of course we have our own dichotomies, because we are not yet merged into oneness. Although some of you believe we are at a higher state of evolution. Perhaps this is the case. In any case it is a different experience in our realm that is sure.

What we want to impart to you now is something about this

experience of greater light for the individual soul, for the individual self experience. What it means to be in light. Outward light shows us a greater perception of things. As a human being, you can see more when there is light. Those of you with shamanic resources can see in the darkness also. Generally speaking for humankind perception is enhanced by light.

What is it that you perceive? If the sunlight is to shine (or the moonlight) very strongly on a trash heap, what you see might not be very pleasant to your eyes. Similarly, just because we are entering a time of greater light, does not mean that what you see will always be pleasing. It means that you have a greater capacity now to understand the truth you are in, to understand the moment you were in, whatever that may be, on an individual soul level. You can "see" more clearly, similarly to how you can see more clearly in daylight than in dark.

Now it becomes your responsibility. Now that you can see more clearly, what do you make of this? Can you take the time to perceive what is there that you could not see or understand before? First, the step is just to perceive it. To notice it is there. To notice that you have skills of perceiving, not always through sight, that were not there before. This is the gift of this eclipse: seeing on an individual level more than you could in the past. Letting go of a certain type of attachment toward dark, toward the unknown. There is a beautiful security and safety floating in the dark unknown because you do not then have personal awareness or responsibility for those things you are not aware of.

So your responsibility widens now with greater sight, with greater perception. And yes we do use sight as a metaphor here. We do not mean that your physical eyes have improved because of this eclipse. We do mean that your powers of perception are greatly enhanced. What does this mean? You may certainly notice truths about your own life, about people around you, about the politics or environment you're in that are quite obvious now that you did not notice, did not perceive, in the past.

So what has happened? The world around you has not changed so much. Of course it has changed drastically in this year, but in this day of the eclipse the world around you has not changed so much, as that you have changed, your ability to perceive it has changed. So some of you will experience now this radical shift of this New Earth that many, many seers and profits and the like have been speaking about. Now you understand what is the big hoopla. Now you understand what it means to you as an individual soul. So we give you this gift of a little extra understanding of what the gift of the eclipse is for you personally.

Why is an eclipse—which is a time of greater darkness—about light? Some eclipses are about dark. But this particular eclipse is about the light of the individual soul. It has to do with a combination of planetary energies and galactic energies at this moment in your universe. It is a shifting toward greater personal light. That means each of you now carry also a greater responsibility. Along with the greatening powers of perception comes the question: what do I do now that I can see more clearly? What do I do with the situation I find myself in?

Understand, please know, that you are never given sight without the ability to respond to what you see. So if you did not perceive these things in the past, it is because you were not ready. Now you are ready, you are given this gift of knowing you are ready for what the greatening light spills out upon in your vision. What does this beautiful dawning light show you? And why is it showing it to you now? Because you as an individual soul are ready to perceive it. With great love this light is given unto you. With great unbounded love.

# VIOLENCE AND DESPAIR

## ANGEL RAPHAEL

*I*t appears that it is a time of more violence and despair, and yet the messages coming from angels and others are that this is the time of freedom. So what is happening here? Both are true.

There are these interferences—let us call them—of violence and despair. As those enslavement mechanisms, no longer in place, those forces which would wish to control humans against their better nature are fighting back a little more strongly now. So it is true there is this seeded despair and violence happening in many small eruptions around the planes of existence where you live at this time.

And yet what is different is—violence has existed for much of human history—what is different is now it is not part of the enslavement. It is a last attempt to re-enslave a free people. Let us explain what we mean by this. Humans have not had a choice, truly, for many, many generations and beyond–have not had a choice about participating in their own destinies in any true sense because they have been entrapped in many mechanisms of enslavement and control. These hidden forces, ruling elites of various kinds, were controlling humans for the most part without them knowing this was the case. In that case eruptions of violence were—let us take Hitler for an example—were quite mechanized, were quite thought out and planned, and humanity was enmeshed in the net of enslavement and had no choice but to follow on one side or the other of this great war. Now what you see are little conflicts. Although they can be quite violent and devastating to those involved, you see they are quite short-lived and localized.

These are not the global wars of the past. Why? Because humanity is no longer enslaved and required to respond with violence. So each parent who had a child lost in a school shooting violence, for example, has the free will and choice to decide: Do I use this for peace and the betterment of society, humanity, or do I choose to have a violent response myself? And you will see that many, many of these parents are choosing peace. Why? Because they have the choice now to do so.

So you will say: There have always been people who were responding against the pull toward war. For the Vietnam War, for example, those who did not want to join the draft forces. Yes. This was one of the first waves of resistance to enslavement, as the energies began to shift on your planes of existence. Before this time there has been very little choice in the matter. In the wars of Europe when Protestants were killing Catholics and vice versa, or when the masses where killing the ruling elite (royalty), there was very little choice in the matter, and you did not see conscientious objectors, what you saw was you were on one side or the other of a battle.

Of course there will always be exceptions to this—deep thinkers, philosophers, and those who remove themselves from conscious mind control. But they were very few at that time. And now they are many. You have many, many people who are sharing these doubts about mechanisms of control and are beginning to be believed on a wider scale. Look at this questioning with what is happening with the uses of internet. These things were not questioned in the past.

We tell you there is a great waking up to the possibilities within this new freedom. At the same time, those forces that no longer have mechanisms (global systems of power, so much gridwork) in place to enslave humanity, are fighting back to try to re-assert some pockets of control. So, as a human now, with free will, it is always your choice to respond with violence or to respond with peace.

Do you wish to be re-enslaved into this game of violence which leads to more violence which leads to more violence? Or do you wish to step back from this cycle and remain free? It is truly your choice. Each individual must make this choice for their own sake and for the sake of humanity. The more that choose this freedom, the more freedom there will be for all. For even those who remain deeply asleep to their freedom at this moment, when enough people have become aware of it they too like the hundredth monkey, they too, like quantum entanglement, they too, like the all-that-is, begin to become aware of their own freedom. So your choice in responding to these moments/pockets of violence is quite important. It is important for your own freedom and it is important for the freedom of all humanity.

Please, we would counsel you—our advice, angelic advice, is to allow this freedom to blossom and grow on these plains of existence and to do your part to let the freedom be very deeply rooted where once enslavement was deeply rooted. Please do your part to ensure that freedom remains here. Please do your part to ensure that each human remembers they have a choice. How you do this is by remembering that you have a choice. In each moment with what is presented to you, you have a choice of how to respond.

Then you begin to see that you have a choice of which moments to create, also. This is the higher learning beginning to descend now onto these planes of existence. Some few, as we have said before, had access to these higher knowledge places in the past already, but it was not so widespread as we are coming into. We are coming into a great time of renaissance, let us say, of global knowledge, of awakening to our freedom. Of awakening to our power of choice.

Right now in this moment it is your choice, both how to respond and how to create your own life choices.

You are both the one ordering from the menu, and the one creating the menu. So start with ordering, if creating feels too weighty for you just now. Start with realizing that you have a choice and that it is your duty to remain free. It is your duty to exercise this choice and not fall into despair. Despair is one of the mechanisms, along with violence, of enslavement. So recognize it for what it is. It is not your nature. It is not a true response. It is an entrapment, an enslavement. Both of these—violence and despair—are an apparent dead end when choice is really there. What you are facing is not the truth of your nature. What you are facing in those moments—violence and despair—is not what you are. You have the choice to lift out of that and choose peace and choose love and choose wholeness and fulfillment and fullness in who you are. You have a choice in this moment to be quite powerfully free.

## YOU ARE THE LIGHT YOU SEEK

### ANGEL ARIEL

We bless you with the understanding that you are the light you seek. If you are the light you seek, there is no distance between what you want and what you are. We had not spoken yet of distance. This is also an ingredient that is no longer essential between you and what you wish for.

So if you are already the light that you seek within yourself, there is nowhere to go to find it. And there's nowhere else you need to appear in order to come into resonance with your own light. So please be assured that where you are right now is where you are meant to be. The opportunities that are available to you right now contain within them what you wish for. You do not have to seek for years to get to some other place, to some other circumstance. You're there right now.

No matter how many times you fell on your face wanting this thing, right now it is accessible to you. Please be assured that in your own light is everything you seek. In your own light is everything that you already are.

There is no journey to take to get to where you are going. That is the old paradigm. Right now you are there. You are at a crossroads with unlimited signposts. And all you need to do is choose where you want to go, and you are there. There's no more long journey. There's no more arduous path.

You have what you seek in front of you. It is just yours to choose it and receive it. Those are the two steps in this process. Choose what you wish. And then receive it.

Your angels are here to help to facilitate that. And more than anything to let you know that you already are that. And that it is completely accessible to you. Whatever it is that you will. As long as you are not wishing harm to any other, anything you want is yours—in this lifetime, in this time, in this physical body, in this circumstance, without any additional time or money or effort on your part but knowing in your heart what it is that you want.

# PART III
# WISHING & RECEIVING

# IT'S TIME TO RECEIVE

## ANGEL ARIEL

It's time to receive what you wish for. Why is it receive and not generate? Generate involves knowing how, taking some action, and creating in a 3D kind of way. Making it happen.

Receiving is just: "Oh wow, what a nice surprise." Receiving is just allowing it to come to you. So that is the time we're in. It's not that you misinterpreted what the world was like two years ago; it is truly a different world now. For all of humanity, there has been such a shift that we invite you to experiment with this belief, your own beliefs about what is possible. And just see. You do not need to believe angel Ariel or even that this is truly angel Ariel speaking right now. But test it out for yourself. Be a scientist and see. You don't need to listen to any external voice. Truly now more than ever, you are the voice that is driving your universe, that is creating it, in truly impossible ways.

The way to experiment with this is to decide about something that you want. And that's really it. It's a one-step process. Decide about what you want, and then receive it. So it's a two-step process [laughing].

*Q: What's the process of receiving?*

Thank you. What if you decide what you want is a six-foot-tall blonde woman to walk through the door and be in your life for the rest of your life? And then the six-foot-tall blonde woman walks in the door? Do you say: "Oh, hello, wow, you really are here!" Or: "I think I'm going crazy. That must be just like a coincidence." Receiving it is also . . . there is some belief here.

Start to pay attention to what you might call synchronicities, or just surprises, beautiful surprises. Particularly look for what looks like collapsed time, like what used to look like it would take 40 years of hard work to get that house or whatever it was, the place on the beach that you want so much, or that vacation time. The mind wants to say if you want that you better be ready to wait. We're not asking you to put timeframe or "how" in there at all, just "what" do you want, and look for things that appear so fast it doesn't make sense.

Let things not make sense to the rational mind. The rational mind is no longer in charge here, unless you put it in charge. So that is the danger here, that if you let the mind continue to believe things are the way they always were it can recreate that for you. So play and experiment. Okay, today I'm going to do the mind way how it usually goes and then tomorrow I'm just going to make wishes and see what happens. Let them be big or small, it really does not matter. And see how your world is going to reorient around what you want. Because now we are come into free will.

The whole purpose of free will is, in a loving way, what are we here to learn or exchange on this planet? We were not meant to come into this life, humankind, as perfected beings who just sit in a corner perfect with themselves, and then leave one day when the body gets old. There must be some reason. Of course, you can reorient this and make your world different. But we would say in general, there must be some reason why humankind is here all together in such a topsy turvy world where people have such distinctly different experiences. Why would that be?

Let's suppose for a moment from an angelic perspective—and humans have different perspectives and galactic races who come in with a lot of wisdom have different perspectives, so you can hear them all or not hear them as you like—the angelic perspective on this is humans came together in this place as a learning planet. This plane of existence, Earth, whether it is 5D, 7D, 3D . . . here on what you call Earth, is a place of such tremendous potential for growth and transformation. If you could imagine in some of the dimensions—disembodied dimensions, so in between lifetimes, the places you go to rest—some of them are quite blissful. So why would any being leave floating in bliss, some equivalent of being in a spa for all of eternity? Why would any being choose to leave that?

Well, maybe the soul wants to grow. Maybe the soul wants to know how to be more compassionate. Maybe the soul wants to experiment with being more magical. If you have decided to be born this lifetime, at this moment on this Earth, it is quite likely that you're interested in your own magic, your own way of being a magical being. And we do not mean spells or incantations. Of course, those are available. But that's a harder way of getting there. We mean just wishing and having your world orient around you.

You do have this ability to use this lifetime to learn, to grow, to transform in ways that are not available in other dimensions and other planes of existence. Because this was set up as a learning, growing experiment. For those of you who liked school, you could appreciate the value of learning. For those of you who don't, perhaps you need some other words around this. Perhaps it is more about achieving, achieving more on the soul level. But of course we do not mean material things, but those achievements of soul that you can carry with you into other dimensions, into other lifetimes.

∼

*Q: Once we receive what we wish for, how do we express gratitude?*

We would say in this context, because it is so new—this wishing and receiving—the best way is to reinforce is to receive that, to believe it. When you do that, each time you take a step of wishing and receiving, you're reinforcing for your soul system here, energetic system: "Oh, this is how it works now. It can be this easy. And it doesn't need to involve so much struggle and strife, so much oppression."

So yes, gratitude of the heart can be there. But even more necessary is to make this new pattern of belief in order for it to keep happening easier and easier. What you will find is you come into resonance with this new way of being. It's not that you should expect yourself all to have graduated from the School of Receive What You Wish the day that you embark upon it. Just start playfully and not expecting so much of yourself, and then reinforce when it happens. Just remember: "Oh, I wished for this and it came. It can be like that." Even more than some ceremony of gratitude of the heart, just relearn this new way. Because we as angels and those guides around supporting you want you to get this, want you to know that the time has changed. And it's okay to wish for what you want now. Even if it's the same wish that you had when you were three or four and were discouraged your whole lifetime, and your mind knows it's not possible. Especially sometimes those wishes. That's the way to break free from this old conditioning. So the best way to show gratitude is to be in that resonance and let that build as if you were a student at school learning how to receive better and better.

You might have a wish. And then it happens. But you don't credit yourself for having made it happen. Because it's not possible [for the wish to come true] in a day. It just doesn't make sense. There will be a lot of that. Getting what you wish for, but thinking: "I don't think it's because I wished for it though, I think it's because it just happened. I knew it was coming." Or you'll come up with some excuses to make it not so easy like it is. It just takes time to relearn how things work.

# CREATING YOUR WORLD

## ANGEL ARIEL

After a little while—so take this with a grain of salt because angels do not live in your linear time—let's say three or five years to give a very general idea, after this wide open, people begin to form communities around ways of thinking. Those beings that want to play with all the galactic beings might start making cities where galactic beings are very visible, for example. Other beings over here have no desire to have that in their reality because it's too threatening, they won't even be aware of these intergalactic cities. Truly there will be so many worlds here on Earth. You know this, you know in your mind that as many people are sitting in a room now that you are having 20 different experiences of the same words. So you know this on some level. It will become much, much more concretely so.

We spoke of the chaos and dipping in and out of third and five dimension we'd like to speak a little bit about this. The words are not so important. Someone asked about how many dimensions are there? The answer, this is Ariel, is it is up to you to decide. Things are not concrete in the way they have formed, even in the rules of the physics of the universe. So you can also recreate that according to your making, according to how you wish it. Then others who kind of like what you created over there can come and play with you in those new dimensions. And those that aren't interested will stay with seven or whatever prescribed levels they believe are available to them.

Because here is where the mind comes into such strong importance. If you believe you are stuck, if you believe that it must be the way it was in the past, you are taking that as a command, the universe is taking that as a command: "Oh, stay stuck. Things must be as they were before." Truly changing your belief in what's possible is the only key here that we would say, perhaps the key message of this talk. It is not that you need to learn some kind of magic or some way of "How do I travel between the dimensions?" or "How do I get there?" But what is necessary is for you to believe what is possible for you. Because even though the door is open, it is free will. No one's going to push you through. So it really is up to your belief of what is possible.

~

*Q: How long will this time of freedom last?*

Understand that angelic time is quite different. We don't believe in time. But we can say generally, we believe from human eyes what this looks like is about three to five years of this wide, wide open playing field. And then, so some have spoken about this split into two Earths. Without getting too technical here, too New Age, let us say we see it as more than two different realities because of this freedom. What happens quite naturally, because humans are creatures of habit, after deciding, playing around with wishes and deciding, let's say in my world, I don't want violence. And I want this blonde. And whatever it is. You might feel like you've come to some synergy with this world you've created and you don't feel the need to have so much disruptive change all the time—every week, something different, a new universe. So as things settle down a little, as people gravitate towards what they want, then you see these groups forming. Here's a group who loves to talk and argue about politics. So their world might still be very political, the way the world is largely speaking now. Whereas maybe all the other groups of people are completely ignoring this political arena. It's very similar to that.

You see this in politics right now, Democrat, Republican, or whatever the split is, there's no sign on the door that says "only Republicans may enter here." But you still find that these people are naturally gravitating towards separate rooms, separate conversation, separate ways of thinking. Like that, the way we see humanity moving right now—and again, it's free will so it can change—it looks like people are going to move into different groupings. We spoke before of the galactic cities, so some that want to be really wide open to meet people, races from other planets. Some who want it exactly how it is today, because that's more comfortable.

We do see that there will be a little bit less movement between dimensions, between ways of thinking, once people find the new normal, the new comfort for them. And it's not because the doors are closing. It's not because you need to run and figure out how you want to make your world before the window of opportunity shuts. The window of opportunity will remain open. But because human creatures like sameness and like habit, after so much chaos and change, and moving dimensions, most people are going to want to settle down for a little while, enjoy the new reality, and maybe not make so many changes. But some among you will want to change every few years. And that will still remain open. So very, very similar to the political discussions now, people will just begin to stay mostly with people who think like them, who want to create the kind of world they want to create. But you can change parties at any time.

## DROPPING MONEY AS AN INTERMEDIARY

### ARCHANGEL RAPHAEL

There are a few layers to this. One is, money itself has been used as one of the enslavement mechanisms for humankind in this three-dimensional Earth plane, in part of this historical experiment. We will give you some shorthand clues here that you might want to follow-up with. One is the Lemurian understanding that you have within yourself full abundance to create anything directly. Complete abundance.

If you overlap this with the enslavement of money, instead of your natural abundance to create for yourself a new house, for example, now here is this system of enslavement that says: "Oh you want that? Well you better work for 40 years and earn this much money then you can have a house." When truly within your own energetic system, you could have created that instantly.

That is one layer, to know that money itself is one of the enslavement mechanisms used in the third-dimensional plane and it is something that those of you who break free into other planes of existence will not carry with you, because it is not needed to impede the sort of instant manifestation of what it is you actually want. It has been described as just a neutral way of barter, but truly it was created as a way of enslavement: "You must have this thing, this money thing, in order to get what you want." When all along humans have had this innate capacity to create what they want, and full abundance within themselves for that. Money in itself is not something we would advise you to strive for, especially now as you are leaving the three-dimensional plane of existence.

Another layer to this: as people disconnect from three-dimensional reality, they become less able in a sense to use those tools—like money, like work—that have been used as enslavement. So there can be a period of time where things seem to get worse on the three-dimensional plane. Money and work seem elusive. The ways of being that were so easy before in terms of manifesting in that realm become difficult.

There is a reason for that. You are disconnecting from those old enslavement systems of slavery so they don't work for you anymore. That is a positive thing but can feel disruptive in the short-term. Long term, understand it is because you are reclaiming your ability and right to instantly have what it is that you desire and want, instead of going through these passageways that are meant to delay what you desire indefinitely into the future, so that you can continue a distracted worker bee.

That is not meant to be your destiny any longer, so those ways of work and money might seem more and more elusive. But that does not mean that you're coming into a time of less abundance. It means that you are shortcutting that system now and going directly to what it is that you wanted in the first place.

That might feel a little bit uncomfortable if you are looking to measure it by bank accounts, number of jobs, and ways you have measured it in the past. But if you step back and look at what is happening truly in your awareness in the last few months, you might see that things are happening differently than you expected, and yet the abundance is there. The food or the house or the friends or whatever it is that you wanted in the first place is coming in a different way and not through the money channels.

You will begin to see when you need something, for example new blankets for your bed, it might not be that you earn the $100 or $40 for the blankets. It might be that someone gives you blankets. It can be much more direct. Money stops being the intermediary between you and what you want.

Playfully you will begin to see this play out—how things just come to you, opportunities just come for you. If you wanted a vacation, maybe instead of needing to pay for it someone had two weeks in their timeshare they're not going to use and they're going to expire, so would you like it at no charge? Things like that, where experiences or things you want can come to you without money coming into the picture at all.

That is what you're moving into. In the transition stage if you're feeling the need for more concrete money, tangible money, look for projects or little spurts of inspiration in that direction, rather than looking for a long-term plan that involves these old enslavement types of ways of working and earning salary.

It will become more and more like that, where things just appear when you want them instead of working for them. It is full abundance. This is just the transition period, where that is understood intellectually, and sometimes experienced dramatically, but not masterful [in] a day-to-day experience. But it will get to that place where it is quite easy.

~

MONEY IS VERY, very firmly in the third dimension. Which means as you move out of the third dimension, you don't need it. It's as simple as that. So again, this can provoke some panic, if things seem different and you're thinking: Wait a minute. Why isn't my life centered around work and money, and that kind of drudgery, slavery work anymore?

Should it be? Should I be trying to struggle to get back to focusing on money all of the time? Of course, that's your option. But we would suggest here that money is very, very much a thread of third-dimensional reality. So as you play in these other fields of existence, you began to understand how much it is true that you absolutely do not need it.

It depends on where you view—the glass is half full, or the glass is half empty. You can see it as you will have less money. It might begin to look like you have less work, less money. But if you are to look from our vantage point, or from more fifth-dimensional reality, when you don't need money for a transaction, you have wealth beyond imagining. You are no longer limited to the coins in your bank account.

This can be viewed from a poverty standpoint, or it can be viewed from an unlimited standpoint. As you get more and more comfortable with the explanations or the physical demonstrations of how you actually don't need money in your world, it becomes less and less fearful to let go of it, and you can be more and more in the joy of the freedom of that free floating, zero gravity again. You don't need that anchor of money. It was holding you back.

## HOW CAN I AFFORD WHAT I WISH FOR?

### ANGEL RAPHAEL

*T*he question arises: How can I afford what it is that I wish for? This is an interesting moment because we find ourselves no longer chained to the domain of money, and yet in most of your world things are still purchased through funds. So how do you decide how to create what you wish? Are you supposed to decide based on what your budget is and what you think you can afford? We tell you that is the old way. But we are not asking you to jump into situations in which you will be chained to the need for money that is not in your current supply.

To jump from a studio apartment to a five-bedroom house just because you want it without the funds available—if you are not yet in a masterful position with this way of wishing and receiving—could put you in a bind of accumulating debt, which chains you then more to the need for money, which you are trying to be free from in this moment in Earth's history.

So how do you make the leap then? You want perhaps more space than in your studio. You want more light, or a safer environment or something like this, or to move to another state but you don't have the money for airfare and shipping your belongings—so how do you make that leap? It comes with trust, yes. But most importantly it comes with specificity of wishing.

What is important for you to have in your mind and your heart is not the price of something. We ask you to discount that entirely when you are wishing. In this case, perhaps you are wishing for five bedrooms, because you have family who wants to live with you. You are wishing for green light—light filtered through trees or something like this. And you are looking for a lake to boat and swim. You have this in your mind. You don't know how financially you could get there. But you do know what you want. This is the important thing: to be clear about what you want. Then what happens: in your email the next day someone says to you: "This summer vacation property is looking for a manager. It comes with a house. It's really only busy in the summer and quiet during the winter but they want someone there all year round to manage and watch this property. Would you be interested?" It comes like this.

We are not saying that the answer to every housing situation is that you will be a caretaker of some kind. But that you will know when your wish has been granted when it comes as a complete package. Meaning, that either you had thought of that thing and suddenly much more money comes your way, and now you know what it is you are going to spend it on, or a situation arises that doesn't involve money in a way you can't quite understand yet. And you don't need to. You don't need to manage those details. In fact, the more you can release from how this will be intertwined with money, the better it will be for you. The easier this can manifest. Just come into great clarity: what it is that you want.

As long as your wishes are not involving dominion over others or harming others—humans, animals, plants and so forth, or galactic beings certainly—as long as you are not wishing harm to others this can appear quite, quite suddenly after you wish it. Begin with this practice of becoming quite focused in your wishing. Then what arises will surprise you.

## CREATING FROM THE HEART CENTER

### ANGEL RAPHAEL

We wish to speak with you today about creating from the heart center. Although the physical heart is a little bit off center, we wish to speak to you about creating from the center of your being—what we would call the heart.

In many, many millennia for this and many lifetimes that you have experienced on Earth, if you have been here before, and certainly in your childhood in this lifetime, the rules were that we were functioning here according to mind. Mind was king. You made a plan. You had a goal. You set out to achieve something and whether or not you achieved it was based on whether or not you followed through on action steps towards your plan. This is the world as it was set out for us as children. Not to say that this is always how it worked in reality; but this is how we were taught the world works.

Now in this last year or so we have come on Earth into a fundamental shift of being-ness. Now the heart reigns. The heart is the one who decides now, how we move forward in our life. What you believe in the core of your heart is what happens for you in your life. That is why we feel it is important to bring you this message, because if you believe in your heart that only bad things happen to you, or you believe in your heart that you are miserable, you can certainly create that for yourself.

We would wish for you to create consciously what you wish to have. And to know that you have the power to manifest that in your own lifetime, and certainly to influence also the scope of humankind and our learning here. Some of you in the room are more concerned with globally as a planet, how do we survive? How do we learn together and uplift through this somewhat rocky time on Earth? You can contribute the most in this time now on Earth, not from the mind space but from the space of the heart.

What do you wish it to look like? And truly that is what appears before you quite naturally and effortlessly. It is very, very similar to how when you pick up your telephone device and you think of someone's name, and you call their number, you reach them. Very, very similar, when you are in the space of creating—which is really always whether you're conscious or unconscious of it—when you call out to a certain energy, to a certain situation in your life, that is what comes towards you. That is what answers.

But we are hesitant to use this word "manifest" because it has been used in decades past to think about either some alchemical spiritual situation, or something you are creating with your mind—through vision boards, through creating and thinking and making action steps. But now on Earth, it is so easy to create from the space of the heart. All you need to do is be clear about what you wish. That is the first, second third and hundredth step in this process of creating through the heart. Be clear what you wish. And that is all. Truly the universe and the angels are ready to organize ourselves behind you and in front of you to help this to blossom forth as you wish it.

What does creating from the heart space mean? It means that this world, dears, is your own creation. It means it is unlimited. This is not a planet, as you have come to think of it, with limited resources and people with different skills and anything else that the logical mind might tell you about where you are. It is much, much closer, the best description we can give is like a holodeck on Star Trek, or some show like this, where your world is literally of your creating. And it seems that real to you.

You are creating what happens in your world. So if you are not happy with exactly how your world is right now, we invite you to change it. And the way to change it is to in the quiet space of your heart—whether that is in meditation or contemplation or perhaps on a walk by yourself—to ask the heart: "What is it that I want? What gifts do I really want to be offering here to humanity? What experiences do I want to draw towards myself?" If you like to start with something that feels more tangible, and perhaps bite size, then: "What quality do I want to bring into this day?"

For example, you might say: "Today, I wish to experience laughter." And then see what shenanigans unfold in your day before you to produce laughter. So it does not have to be a weighty thing. You do not have to change the names of the continents and things like that, to prove to yourself that this works. Because that probably is not what you really care about most in your heart space. Go there and ask the heart: What does it want? And once you are clear, just stay with that knowledge of what your heart wants, and be amazed at how the world unfolds from there for you.

Your experience of the world may be very, very different than your neighbor's. Someone may talk to you endlessly about how the world is becoming so violent and awful, and this and that. And you might thing: "Really? Because all I see are angels. It's an amazing time to be alive!" And both are true, because you are creating your own world from your heart space. And you can draw towards yourself those evidences, those experiences, to prove yourself correct.

The other thing we wish to say today is ask for help in this. When you learned to drive a car, you probably did not just encounter a car for the first time, get in, and figure out as you went how to drive it. Similarly, realizing that you are the creator of your own world may be old news to some people, but might be quite new to you. So ask for help. You have guides and angels around you. You can ask for guidance to appear in the form of books, in the form of video talks, in the form of friends, in the form of meditation . . .however you wish to receive knowledge, you can ask for it. That is part of being able to create what you want in your heart space. You are not being flung into the deep end to learn how to swim here. But it is more like you are waking up and realizing the whole planet is made up of water. So: "Oh, what is this swimming thing I'm supposed to be doing?" As a metaphor. We do not see the world being engulfed by water, for those of you with literal minds.

∼

*Q: How do you deal with doubt? Where you're not sure if that's your heart talking. How can you tell?*

Doubt is the language of the mind. So one of the first clues, if you feel doubt, is that is not your heart speaking. The heart is very sure of what it wants. The mind has become uncertain that you can actually have that thing. And that is where the tension comes. Because you wish for something but then the mind comes in and says: "I don't think I'm supposed to want that." Or: "I don't think that's possible." The doubt comes from the mind. And because the mind has been in charge for many millennia, it is quite used to being the one in the driver's seat. So it is up to you to gently say: "Wait a minute, this doesn't sound like my heart. I don't think what I want to be creating is a whole list of stressful reasons why this can't happen." So take a few deep breaths then, and really wait in silence for the heart to speak. It is a softer voice, and yet it is very sure what it wants.

This will be quite new to some of you to live from the heart. Know that in a broader sense—because as much as it is our own universe to create, we are also interacting with other people and their universes— the Earth itself, the energetic structures here are now in support of this creating from the heart space. There were those who knew how to do this thousands of years ago. It is not new. But it used to be the purview of those priests and yogis who had practiced quite fervently to reach this place. Now it is available to all of us. But we are not all yet aware that it is a power that we have.

∽

*Q: How do we break from the past so that we don't create from that space?*

Why do people seem to create the same situation over and over? Have you noticed that you have a good friend who leaves a job that they hate, and two months later, they have found themselves somehow in the exact same situation in another job? Which is mysterious to you, because in your whole life, you have never encountered such a thing. So like that, yes, there is this tendency to create in circles. That is how the mind creates. Because the mind feels very sure about what it knows is true. And so it will keep creating that even though your spirit and other parts of you want to break out and create something new, your mind didn't believe it. So it creates that track again. So how do we get out of this circular creation of the mind?

The heart—you might find if you spend some time meditating with it, and being in the heart—is much more a thing of the present moment. Although grieving can be a way of expressing from the past, if you were to ask the heart what it wants, it is not going to tell you what it wanted one lifetime ago. But the mind might be remembering that. The heart is a creature of the present moment, which is why this manifesting of the heart seems many times almost instantaneous, and in ways that completely defy logic.

Trusting that, in the past if you have created something that came back into your life again, or a person that seems like they couldn't quite cycle out of your life, trust now that your heart has the support of a very different energetic system behind it—on the Earth itself, and in the atmosphere, so to speak, around it. And the interplanetary connections as well for those who are more multi-dimensional beings. We do not want to get too technical, but just to say that there are so many supports now for this different way of being. So that even if 10 years ago you tried something similar, it is not the same moment.

If a baby tried to walk just out of the womb, they would find it quite frustrating. They probably do, which is what some of the crying is about. Later on, when the legs are formed, it's an easy thing. So we're in that phase of life now where it's an easy thing to create from the heart. We ask you not to prejudge your experience based on what happened a year or 10 years ago, and to just experiment.

You will know quite quickly if this works or not. There is no reason to believe this message or anyone else if your experience does not prove it to be so. So try it out. Experiment with things that are tangible enough that you can tell if they happen or not. And learn this muscle of the heart and how effortlessly it manifests what you want. It truly is not stuck in the past. Even the emotions that express through the heart most often—and this is nuanced, of course for each person—but most often greed or a feeling of unfairness might be in the mind, and grief might be held in the body cells. Those things that are of the past are not truly in the heart in the present moment. So we do not create from those past wounds. Even if we are still aware of them. We do not create from that place.

## CREATING NEGATIVE—OOPS!

### ANGEL RAPHAEL

*L*et's speak about creating negative things. Because we've been speaking about wishing and receiving. But the truth and the trap here, when you are such a strong creator being as all of you are, is that you can also create negative circumstances by believing in them.

That's when you repeat before you leave the house: "It's always impossible to find a parking spot at this location." And you get there, and there's no parking spot. You have the ability to create negative things as well. When you find that you're doing that, or if you find yourself in fear or doubt or worry, just when you recognize it, catch that it is happening. Understand that this also could be seen as positive; this is a demonstration to you of how you are creating your world. Because you can change it instantly, just stop in that moment when you recognize what you've been doing—creating from a fear space, or from habit space—"Agh, this is something that always aggravates me." Is that what you want?

If it's not, then create something positive out of that situation. It could be in the form of a wish. For example: "Okay, I'm going to this place where I've felt so frustrated in the past. Today, I'd really like to just have an easy experience with parking." It can be that simple. You're not pretending that the past doesn't exist. But recognize that you are under no obligation in any area of your life to repeat the past.

Just because you believe in something very strongly, it has a very three-dimensional pull on you. It's something that feels so real, like money, like work, like aging and death. What if you had the ability to change these things? What if you had the ability to perceive things in a more "real" way? What if you recognize that when this body dies, you are in no way dying? You come to approach death, then, in quite a different way. Perhaps just respecting that this body, physical body that you're wearing, right now has some limitations. And you have the ability to also help the body through your wishes. You know, you're already immortal.

These kind of negative concepts that you believe in for a while are most often false, or they're just something you created because you believed in it. It happened a few times so you made that mental note: "This is the way the world is." And the world then responds: "Well, she told us this is how she wants the world to be." So just wake up in that moment and say: "Oh, wait! That's not how I want the world to be. I thought it had to be that way." No. Really, for all of the circumstances in your life it is that magical.

And when you trip up and get it wrong, and forget and get in that old groove about: "It's always impossible to find a parking place here," you can also just laugh in that moment and recognize what you're doing. "Oh my gosh, I am so powerful in creating my world. And I've been creating the same frustrating story over and over again." And maybe that was more real, maybe I was more stuck in that when I was limited to the third-dimension. But I'm not anymore. I really do not have to play that game any longer.

This is a time of playing. You don't have to know. You don't have to know how it works all at once. But you do have tremendous ability to change your life now, to change your world. Please do use those skills playfully. Just experiment with what it is you think you want. And when it comes to you accept it like that. "Oh, this is something I wanted. I could at least try it. And then if I don't like it, I could wish for something else."

But get in the habit please of wishing and then receiving what you wish for instead of receiving doubt. Meaning, when your wish comes thinking: "Uh oh. Was this my destiny? Was I supposed to choose something else? Did I make the wrong choice?" Be a little more playful dears with your lives right now. And you can be serious later, if you like, once you understand how this works. Once you use trial and error to create some new circumstance in your life. Be playful.

Even in those times when you forget, use that as a sign to yourself about how this works, how it is possible also to create what you fear, what you believe to be true. But that doesn't mean you're bound by it. The second you recognize that's what you've been doing, you're in that powerful moment where you can change it—without any particular technique except for wishing for what you want and then receiving it, moving in those new directions when it comes your way.

# WISHING FOR HEALTH

## ANGEL RAPHAEL AND ANGEL GABRIEL

*Q: Regarding the importance of specificity when wishing, does that technique also work for healing the body of any ailment? Or does one still need to consult with a healer, doctor or take medication or supplements to assist the body and healing?*

This is Raphael and Gabriel both. We will use an analogy here. If you were just learning to paddle around in a baby pool and you learned about the ocean and thought: "Wow, that must be better," we wouldn't advise you jumping in and being a long-distance ocean swimmer right away on the first day. It is like this with wishing, and we will speak particularly about health.

If you were just starting to experiment with wishing and how powerful it is, you might not want to say today: "All right, I wish to be cured of my cancer," and then do nothing about it on the human physical level. Disband from seeing any doctors, not going to any healers, not getting anyone's advice just saying: "Okay, I wished it, therefore it is." Once you get to a level of mastery with wishing absolutely that is possible. It is available to you.

It is available to you now, but like this metaphor of being in the kiddie pool and then the ocean being available to you, you do need to learn how to swim. You need to learn how this works, this mechanism of wishing. It is not that it is more accessible to some people than others. Or that you are not fully capable of receiving everything you wish right now in this moment; it is not that. But it is a little bit like a skill, something you might practice, the way the first time you go to the gym, it feels quite horrible. And then it builds—your skill, your ability to gain strength from such a thing. We are not saying that wishing will feel horrible, but it might feel awkward and uncertain at first, certainly.

So yes, in all fields—in fields of wealth, in fields of healing—wishing is enough. But here then look at all of the wide field of opportunities you have with interacting. Let's stay with this example of cancer. If you were to wish for health, and then a few minutes later your friend emails you and says: "Wow, I just heard about this great doctor in Waikiki, and you live 20 minutes away. Can you just drive there and visit this doctor? I really think they can help you." Do you say: "Oh, no, no, no, I just wished for the end of cancer. I don't need to see anyone." Or do you recognize perhaps this is the answer to your wish? You're being sent, in many cases in response to a wish, the person who can help you get there, the library book . . . Sometimes it is a material manifestation of light, of healing. But sometimes it is a more playful interaction with others.

So there is no one right answer here to: Do you stop seeing a doctor? Or: What type of doctor should you see? Partly it's up to your choice. And partly it is up to your ability to trust that when you sincerely wish to your angels or whoever you wish to—God, the universe, however you phrase this, the all-that-is—when you place that wish, can you trust that God, the universe, the all-that-is knows how to best answer that wish for your physical, emotional, energetic system? Perhaps your energetic system is not at capacity right now in this moment to receive instant healing. Perhaps you want a three-month Reiki or energy journey which will give you what you need. So being open and trusting to the fact that there are many, many, many modalities of healing, and not all of them are suited to each person at each time. Even what worked for you last week, what has always worked for you. You might have moved on and your energies might have changed enough, be open enough to seeing that magazine article, to hearing that friend's advice that is <u>now</u> the right thing for you moving forward.

# WHAT SHOULD I WISH FOR?

### ANGEL ARIEL

*J*ust because you have the capacity to wish for what you want doesn't mean you need to understand what that is right away. What we are asking is in those situations where you are clear where what you want, whether it's a chocolate bar, or a new job, or a new friend or relationship, or a new way of being a healer in this world—so whatever level of wish, even if it's something very practical and easy to obtain otherwise—when you are clear about what you wish for, then please wish it and be aware you are wishing and then watch out for how you are receiving it. And we don't mean "watch out" in the booby trap sense, but in the sense of just be aware. Watch it coming towards you.

Just for now, while you're not so clear what it is that you want, you can just wait and wish for things when you know what they are. It doesn't have to be 17 wishes every day. It's just that we want you to be aware that this is available to you now. It's not that you have a limited amount of coins here, golden coins for your wishing. So you don't have to be so worried about saving them for when you're really really sure. We would advise to practice, to think of it more as a learning and a practice time than a time of wasting wishes. We don't see small wishes as being frivolous in this time, because they are wonderful demonstrations of how this works. And it builds trust. Then when you are ready to wish for what is very dearly in your heart, you can be at ease with that.

There's no rush about wishing. It's not a limited time window that will close. It's just open now. And we encourage you to play and practice the way you learned tying your shoes. You don't need to take it so seriously. And if there are not big wishes right now, how beautiful. Reflect for a moment how content perhaps you are in your soul that you don't have so many wishes right now. There is a great beauty in that also.

~

*Q: I can't get clear on my wish. I feel conflicted about whether to move or not.*

This is a good example. When there is not clarity about what to wish for, we would say to you: there's no rush. Maybe start a catalog in your mind. These are the things I love about my home. If I were to move, or if I were to stay here, these are the things I enjoy that I would like to replicate or stay the same. These are the things that feel frustrating, and I'm ready to let go of. You don't need to understand in your mind how to reconcile what is the right house then or the right timing for the move. As you get clear on the components of something that you like, and that no longer resonate with you, in a way you're building wishes without realizing that's what's happening. It does help to get clarity about what you want and what you don't want—just the components of it. So you don't have to know it's this exact house in this neighborhood that's going to make me happiest, and I feel like I really know that. I'm ready to wish for it. You can just start observing in your life, what are things that you want either the same or more of, and what are things that you feel like: this element is a little stale, but I don't know when it might be time to move on. It's okay to have those gray areas.

As you move into accelerated times, those things that you have identified clearly as not resonating well with you will naturally fall away, without your having to make the effort or even the wish for that to happen. So it's helpful to your guides to the energies around you—which more and more will feel less like individual guides and more like swirling energy, or energy you are dancing with—it's helpful to that energy, universal energies around you, to know. What are you feeling? I'm discordant with this, I don't really want this anymore, but I don't know how to let go. Or, I don't know why or when, I just feel a little uncomfortable with this piece.

Just catalog that for yourself, please. And know that as things accelerate, the energies around you will find ways to get rid of those things, but not in a violent sense. They will find very peaceful, loving ways of showing you different doorways than you might have been able to conceive of in your mind. Part of what is difficult here with wishing is we're used to doing that with the mind. And the mind, having been familiar, locked in with old systems of ways of being, sometimes isn't the best judge of what to wish for, what's even possible. So it's okay to get partial clarity here. Just start a catalog of: these are the things I'd really like in my life, and these are the things that feel stale. And I have no idea how the newness is going to come together. Just leave it at that.

You don't have to know in this moment what it is you're wishing for. As we had said, the door is not going to close here. You don't have to decide that just yet. It could be that in the ripeness of your soul and the ripeness of perhaps, for example, another free will being who's about to come into your life, maybe they are also not quite ready. So there's a little delay in timing here out of compassion for both of you. And the meeting comes when you're ready, when you both know what you're wishing for.

Allow for grace in this, for the beautiful compassion of universal energies to help you dance with this. And it's all right if you don't feel clear in this moment. Maybe it's not the right time for action. And action in this sense we mean driving the becoming, the "I am" through your wishing, through your understanding of what you are coming into. You can do the research, the preparatory work, for as long as you like. And when it becomes clear: "Oh, I see what are the things that I want now," you still don't need to know how is it going to come to you—financially, or time wise, or logistically speaking. But when you feel clear about what you want, that's the time to make the wishes. You don't need to feel rushed in this.

# RECEIVING QA

## ANGEL RAPHAEL AND ANGEL ARIEL

*Q: How do you overcome that reluctance to just trust yourself that you will pick the right things and create the right life? I feel reluctant because of the power behind this.*

*Angel Raphael:*

We apologize to some of you. What we're about to say might sound quite heavy, and there isn't a less direct way of saying this. For this beautiful soul, we want to answer it this way. If you were trying to enslave a magical being who had the ability to open the door and be free at any time, wouldn't you be whispering in their ear: "Oh, you can't do that. Your choices are bad. Absolutely bad things happen when you wish for things." If you were trying to keep them from wishing for things which were going to come true? It is the enslavement mind that has been telling us for so long "Don't go there, wishes are scary."

We would tell you from angelic perspective, your wishes are safe. As long as you are not trying to harm another. As long as—and we will bring in a Lemurian perspective—as long as you are not trying to hoard someone else's to make it only yours and you never share, all of your wishes are safe. It is as if you were in this friendly holodeck. Even to contradict a little bit our example from a moment ago, you can just create anything you like. It's just a holodeck. It's just a life. You've been here thousands of times before. What if you make a mistake? Have another one! And again this is why we said you don't have one wish or five wishes. It's not some set amount. And you're not locked in. This is what I want right now. And when you get it, you can try it on and say: "Okay, this is almost what I want. But I want to shift this over here." Because how do you know until it arrives to you? There is no angel or universe judging you: "You better figure this out and make one wish and get it right, because that's it, that's all you got." No, you're like a child with colorful paint on your fingers and just play and mess it up and get it wrong and wash your hands and do something else.

*Q: What if I feel blocked?*

*Angel Ariel:*

We want you to know that, especially historically, before two years, one year ago, that barrier was very real. So you have this memory, mental memory, muscle memory of: "I wished for it. I didn't get it. I wished for it. I didn't get it. I wished for it. I didn't get it." And that was true. We're not trying to say you misperceived all that. There was a huge wall that said: no. Now the wall is not there anymore. Here is why the message is so strong to wish for things because you're in the habit now of not wishing, because you kept coming up to that wall which said no. Now just appreciate that now, today is different than it was last year, wildly different, more so than you could conceive. If you were all able to visually—and some of this room can—perceive how much the world is changed, it would be a little much to take in even, how much. It looks the same. The chairs looking the same, your neighbors look the same. There is some compassion there that the change is not so abrupt that we all just fall down on the floor, disoriented. Have the courage to try again, to wish again. And not (with your mind) "know" that it won't happen because it didn't happen these 47 other times. You were correctly perceiving it didn't happen and there was a block there. But we are telling you the block is not there anymore. Have the courage to be that innocent child that just wishes for things.

∼

Q: *How detailed do you need to be?*

*Angel Ariel:*

This is a beautiful question. You were taught to manifest something you had to be so specific and visual, or else it wouldn't happen like that, to magnetize toward that reality. It's not really like that in this time. It had been, that was one method of getting things you wanted in the past. And it's still valid, but a harder way. Again, for some, the details are so delightful. You want someone with that tattoo on the left shoulder. And for some what's important is this broad brushstroke of I just want to feel like this when I meet them.

So really, it's up to you. Are the details important? And is that how you're going to recognize that person, if it's a person you want to draw into your life and receive? Or is it how you feel or how it transforms you? So the wish does not need to be technical, it does not need to be detailed. And it does not need to be visceral in that sense, visual or otherwise. It can certainly be much, much broader. For example: I want to meet someone who's going to (and this does not have to be romantic) give me the key to what my greatest strengths are that I haven't recognized yet. It can be quite vague in that sense.

But you know what you want. You've been trained through experience to stop wanting it because it's painful to keep hitting that wall. But you do each know what you want. It's just allowing yourself to wish again, to be in that beauty of the innocence of a child who says "I want to be an astronaut." And no one in the room is there saying:

"No. That's not possible. You're not old enough. We don't have enough money as a family," whatever it is. There's no one saying no to your wishes right now. So have that. Be that.

～

*Q: Why is it that some things manifest so quickly? And then with other things you're like: "What's going on?"*

*Angel Ariel:*

We talked about the compassion of not being disoriented by so much change all at once. What is also happening is . . . Some of you may have heard and some of you might may not have heard people talk about the old way of being as third dimensional, very concrete: chair, table, must work hard for this. And fifth dimension being much more instant reality, time and space not being an obstacle anymore.

What is happening is humanity has access now to fifth dimension and other dimensions. You sometimes step into, not necessarily consciously trying to, just find yourself in fifth dimension. And one of the hallmarks of that is things happen like that. And then tomorrow morning, you wake up thinking: "Oh, great, this is how the world works now." So you wish for it. And then you just feel tired, and the computer doesn't work and something else . . .

What's happening now is you are in both, usually not simultaneously. To simplify this, let us say as you're walking around you're stepping into third dimension for a few minutes, hours, and then you're over here in fifth . . . And when you're not controlling this consciously, suddenly your energy is playing with these different dimensional realities. It is a little bit back and forth right now.

And part of the reason is compassion to give you an experience what both feel like and the contrast. For some of you this feels quite annoying, because you really like fifth and now to come back into the heavy, heavy of third feels awful at those times. But understand globally for humanity, why it's happening this way is to allow people to play in the new energies, experience the difference, and it might feel for you like totally ungrounded, blissful ether for a few hours. And you don't know why your brain can't think. And then you're very, very grounded the next day. So you're trying to figure out what am I doing differently? It's truly not you right now; it's the planetary energies dancing. And why they're doing this is because it's too stark of a change to just step through: now we're in fifth, no looking back. And part of it is for this free will, so that you can experience both, or the seventh and other dimensions as well are open. Most people are playing in third or fifth right now back and forth. That is meant to be compassionate for humans to try it out, and then even though they love it: "I think I need a nap because that was a lot of energy."

When you're in fifth, you will find wishes and the fulfillment happens so easily like that. And then some days when you're in third and you can't make it work, just don't try to make third work like fifth. You can still make your wishes when you're in third, then you might have to wait a day or two. It's still much more instant than it has been. It's not 40 years, it's maybe next time you're in fifth. Okay, stop by and get that while we're here. There is this interplay of dimensional realities. So do not fear that you missed the boat. If you were feeling this huge expansion last year and then you felt like you came crashing down (or some days you feel that way). Yes, that's what's happening. But it's not because you fell off your soul path or you didn't meditate enough, it's just that the energies are in quite a beautiful chaos right now. But it is meant to be that way to give the human system time to adjust and to choose.

# PART IV
# BECOMING

## YOU ARE IN THE FIELD OF GOD

### ANGEL RAPHAEL

We do not speak in terms of "archangel". We do not speak in terms of a God that is distant from you. Hierarchy in this sense is a very human concept. Not one born of light, pure light.

In light we are one. You are brother or sister with angels.

And we are in the field of God, what you could call God.

We want you to recognize this as you come forward into the fullness of who you are, that you are not striving to be one bright point inside a hierarchy.

You are disillusioning yourself that you were ever anything other than light, fullness of light in all its expressions.

## A TIME OF BECOMING

### ANGEL ARIEL

We want you to know you are in a time of becoming. What does it mean to be in a time of becoming? Are you becoming someone or something else? We think not. But you are creator beings, let's say.

You have entered a new phase of your evolution. And we mean this collectively in humankind, we are in a time now of becoming. So that's a little different than the time of reflecting, where you were a bit of a mirror for what was around you. And it's certainly different than a time of being trodden upon and subjected to someone else's vision for yourself or your life.

What does it mean to step into becoming? And how do you operate this new way of being? You know very well how to follow rules, how to follow orders, how to follow (somewhat begrudgingly perhaps) someone else's vision for yourself. But what does this mean "becoming"?

"I am" is the beginning of the becoming statement. So "I am a dancer," if you are affirming this to yourself, you start to see situations in your life—the classes, the teachers, the time in your schedule, to create such a being, a dancer being. "I am an intellect." Suddenly, those curiosities of your mind, the library books, again the teachers, the friends, come with great clarity.

As you are becoming, as you are making these statements to yourself, to the God within you and around you: "I am ..." and then whatever you are wanting to become into ... your world not just reflects that, but becomes that for you.

You as a creator being now decide what it is that is in your "I am." Some of you are moving towards dissolution of all identities. You might call that the enlightenment process. We don't mean annihilation in a negative sense. But for those of you who are moving towards dissolution of identities, you can just stay with the "I am" or move towards "am" which is the pure reverberation of self. And in "self" we mean that piece of your consciousness that you are responsible for while still being emerged into the all, the God that is.

When you are in this phase of becoming, it's not very important to make lists about "How do I need to get there? How do I need to step into what I would like to become?" It is very important to decide <u>what</u> it is you want to become so that you're not picking up, like radio waves, what everyone else is thinking and feeling and believing about the world. If you were just to sit in front of the television all day or read newspapers and decided to become that, you might feel a little muddy and a little chaotic and perhaps a little unnecessary drama there. So it's good to be clear. What is part of your becoming? What is this "I am"?

It is not that you have one choice here. It is not that you are a creator being with one child and that you are limited then to this "I am" identity for the rest of this lifetime or the rest of the soul's identity. "I am" is as flexible as a kaleidoscope. As flexible as time. It doesn't need to be any more real or longer duration than that. So you can play with this. You don't need to feel that: "Oh dear. Now I'm in this becoming I better learn how to become a creator being and do it very consciously and spend seven years building my new identity." No. You could have an identity for seven minutes if you like. Try it on, and if it doesn't feel right, try something else. Yes, there will be a settling down some years from now—two, three, four years, five years from now—where perhaps you have decided by then what it is that "I am," or perhaps you've decided by then to be "am." So this is the time of more play and experimentation.

Although this creator-ness will still be open to you in the future, it will likely settle down. You'll likely find one or two or three identities that you're happy to stay with in this body in this lifetime. We do see this settling down, but for now we would say be like the child or the adult who just opened the new box of paints and just play. Be a little creative in exploring this please. It's not so serious as you once imagined to create an identity, to be something. When you were in the time in between lifetimes choosing what identity to choose for this lifetime, you didn't, we think, take it so seriously. You recognized this as one lifetime among many. And you made your best choices based on what you knew at that time. So now you've learned and grown over some years, the decades here in this lifetime. And maybe you have some new choices you'd like to make. Maybe you'd like to branch out into different identities than the ones that you chose for yourself coming in. So now is the time of freedom, of exploration, where you can try that out and not feel you need to commit to new long term identities, but just be, practice this becoming.

You see the word "be" is there in "becoming." It's all about the emanations of your being outward. So much so that the universe, the environment, your friends, those other creator beings around you, join with you to create this identity, this becoming. Why would you do such a thing, despite the fact that it is available to you? Why not continue with the identities you have now? Certainly that is a choice for you. So as you look at the unlimited field of potential, one of the choices is to remain exactly as you are. Of course, exactly as you are will still shift moment to moment. But you needn't take a drastic leap into some other identity in order to explore the change and growth that's available to you. It's just an option. And one of the options if you're quite pleased with the choices you've made in forming your identity in this life is to stay with what you have, to continue down the path you had started. Perhaps you feel you have a lot invested, in terms of time and lessons learned, and you'd like to just move forward from here. Absolutely. That is open to you.

What we are saying is: it's up to you. For it was not—generations of your upbringing here on this planet in this lifetime—it was not up to you for some time here. And so now it is, we want you to be aware of the change. We want you to be aware of the freedom, the growth, the huge opening that is for you here.

We welcome you into the maturity of your soul. Understand that as creator beings, you have earned this right to create your world around you. You have already done the hard work. You have already done the apprenticeship. You do not need to doubt yourself so much in creating your world.

Creator beings—yourselves we mean—are not limited to creating one thing, one lifetime. So you don't need to feel that you are making a limited choice, either between limited options, or that you only get one of the unlimited options.

Truly for you in this lifetime, you can experience infinity and growth—infinite growth, infinite abundance and whatever that means for you. But the reason for being specific as you create is "abundance," larger words like this, mean vastly different things to different people. For some people, that means caviar. For some people, that means a tropical climate. For some people, that means I don't have to work. For some people, that means organic food. For some people, that means living under the stars with nothing.

So it's helpful for the universal energies dancing around you to know: what is your language of abundance, of love? What is it that you wish to create, to be, in this moment? What is abundance for you? What is becoming for you?

Part of this journey towards wishing is to understand that although the wishes often now will come quite instantly, that does not mean that you instantly need to be ready to make the wish. It is still the fruition of life that you are moving towards—which has to do with growth, which has to do with soul change. And you get to choose the pace of that. You get to choose how quickly you come into your wishing and knowing what to wish for. You get to choose. Our role here as angels is to let you know what is open to you, which is truly unlimited, to let you know that you are the creator here, not the creation. You yourself are creating what you are. And we want you to feel empowered to fully be that. To fully become that being that you are.

In the fullness of wishing, in the fullness of being what you are, is already the receiving of the wishing. So you do come to a point where the wishes fall away entirely. It is not that the point of understanding you have wishes is to create many wishes, necessarily. You might only have three in this lifetime. There is no need to create a complicated structure in your becoming, in your being in this life. And there is no need for it to be simple, if you like the dance of complexity. It truly is up to you to create this divine desire. And to live it out.

# THE LIGHT COMES FROM YOU

## ANGEL ARIEL

From our perspective, angelic perspective, the light comes from you, dears. It does not come from without, from outside of yourself. Yet, another attribute of the humankinds, you tend to look for light outside of yourself—to call it God, or the Universe, or your Higher Self. But when you say higher self you are often placing this light outside of yourself and trying to come into resonance, into alignment, with this higher self, these higher energies.

It is a bit of a joke, really—and we do not mean this in a cruel sense—but it is comical that you are carrying in a sense this glowing light—the heart of all, the source of all—within yourself and you look outside yourself to find it in the view or another partner, or some other place or time. Often you want to put it also in a future time when you think you'll be more in resonance with your greatest self.

In this exact moment, you are in the core of your being the living light. You are the highest vibration of yourself. You are the highest expression of yourself. Right now, you are the highest expression of what you have to give on this Earth, the highest expression of what you have to receive and belong into.

You are all that you seek in this lifetime, and all of the knowledge you have brought with you, and all of the knowledge you seek to gain in the future. Right now, in the glowing heart of you, is this change you seek. To shed and show more and more of your light into the world. To shed and be aware of more and more of your light glowing outward and inward. This one unidirectional light that is both outside, but mostly within you. You perceive it from the outer physical eyes. You perceive it from the inner heart. And it comes from the deepest place within you. It is not something that you need to grasp and hold on to from outside yourself.

Times like now when you feel this great change upon the Earth—when you feel this great heaviness at some times leaving you but it feels like it is depressing upon you at some times, especially of late—seek within this great light. It brings you stability in times of changes like these. You carry within you everything you need to weather these storms, whether they are temporary blips or huge sea changes of humanity as we are in now. You carry within you the light, the blessing, the strength of this tremendous light. It is not a fairy tale. It is not something outside yourself. It is the core of what you are.

Will you think us apocryphal if we say to you that <u>you</u> are God? We do not see it this way, that God is something outside of each being, that is directing and relating with us. We see God as this light, this core light that connects all of us from within. Sometimes we want to look outside for this guidance of God, for this light of God. But it is within the core of you. It is within the core of each of you. No matter how tarnished or depressed or broken down you think you have become. That is a memory or an illusion, both. It is not the truth of who you are. Bathe right now in the truth of who you are: this brilliant, brilliant light.

See how the light is emanating from you into the pores of your being, of your physical body. Releasing was doesn't need to stay there: memories, old habits of muscle and bone. And coming into that alignment with what you are, that alignment with light. Let all of these physical dis-eases this misrememberings of who you are just shed naturally away and melt into this light emanating from within you. And know that this is the core of your being.

# FINDING LIGHT WITHIN YOURSELF

## ANGEL RAPHAEL

For many of you this idea of finding light within yourselves is attractive, but elusive. It is a nice concept, but you're not seeing light there. Perhaps you're wondering if you're supposed to visually see it, if it's supposed to be a vibration that you feel.

Angels are an expression of light a bit more so than humans are. Again, we do not mean this in a sense of hierarchy, but you are a denser physical being which is why you are feeling this transition so much now as density is leaving in some sense, getting less everywhere. For angels it is easier to express and play in this concept of light. Because we can perceive that in ourselves even in the outward physical sense, when we look at ourselves we perceive light. Do not, please, put this burden on yourself of always needing to understand or grasp how it is that you are light. We can see it in you a little more clearly than you can see it in yourself.

What [do] you do then when you want to come into the core of yourself, this light as we have expressed it, but you can't resonate with that imagery so well, it's not taking you anywhere?

[Some of you] relate better with a sense of expansion-ness. A sense of being like salt dissolving into water. When you want to come into this truth of who you are, into this light within as we have expressed it, you might feel a little more resonant dissolving into the all that is.

For all of you it might be something different. It might be listening to the birdsong, something outside of yourself that lifts you out of the impression of your own heaviness for a moment. It might be submerging into some water or ocean waves. It might be letting sound submerge into you, playing some kind of sounds or vocally toning some kinds of sounds.

There are many ways into, there is not one best way into this experience of your highest light. Whatever it is for you, and it might be different day to day, seek that. For now, we want you to know on a conceptual mental level—because the mind is very, very heavy right now, with this density, this absence of light that is leaving. It is the mind that needs the most convincing right now, that everything is OK. You are not in a fight or flight for your very existence.

It is the mind that needs a little talking to which is why we use what is for some of you a very mental concept of coming into the core of your own being, which is light. Because the mind can relax in this conceptually—light within you as being an unchanging place. So it also feels a little safer as a mental concept. But from our perspective, angelic perspective, this light within you is very real. It is connected to the all-that-is. Which is why some of you perceive it a little better in this relaxed sort of dissolved sense of being in the all-that-is. And some of you perceive it a little better by seeing this beautiful glowing light in your heart—in perhaps not a visual sense, but a felt sense that it is there.

# YOU ARE GOD

## ANGEL ARIEL AND ANGEL RAPHAEL

This is Ariel and Raphael, both. We'd like to leave some energies into this answer for you here. For each of you. This is a fundamental question: Why is it that we did not come into this birth, particularly this lifetime, already knowing that we are God?

Why do we walk around with this illusion that we are not—that we are something separate, alone, afraid, dark, small, fragile, all of these qualities that you believe that you are? Well, in a way, yes, God is all of those things too, because God is expressed here in a polarity. There are the winged creatures, and those that walk on legs, and there are those that seem more fragile, and those that seem more predatory, and so on. In the natural world, you can see these gradations in a more neutral way. But when you see it in yourself, you think of it as this shell of wrong understanding or smallness. We see it as an expression of learning.

Why in this particular moment—the angels are asking you to consider—why in this moment, not generally all the time but why in this moment, do I feel small? Why in this moment do I feel sad? And to hold this question within you as if it were a sacred purpose. As if it were the window into the light that you are. So instead of discounting them as something negative or a burden you must carry, these questions, then, where do they lead you? Hold these questions quite dear, because they are the window out, in a sense, of your light out into the world. And as your light sheds out into the world, it carries with you, through you, this light of understanding, of new knowledge. The questions are the way in (or out, depending on how you look at this metaphor of the light, more light reaching you).

∽

THIS IS ARIEL. The use of religion and spirituality, both, have been used both to uplift and to deter humanity from this sense of direct connection with God. Historically, there have been many instances where churches, other religions, various faiths, have used this concept of priest, of hierarchy, to keep people feeling that they are not allowed to directly access God because they are in sin, or some other reason, some other excuse that they must go through these very specific prayers, very specific priests and rituals in order to come anywhere close. But still, God is really not something accessible. So that has been a trick, a misogynist kind of trick against humankind, by some faiths.

However, there have been some faiths and some religions that did the opposite, that taught people that they are this light and taught people different ways at different historically appropriate times that they are this access point themselves, to light, to what is called God. Sometimes these faiths have been viewed as apocryphal, and sometimes they have been viewed as the highest light, the highest knowledge, depending on the civilization.

So there's not one answer here about religion, given time and place, but we will say that one of the layers that are leaving—one of these dense layers—is this misperception that you are separate from . . . this misbelief: I am not God. This is leaving in a more gentle way. It is one of the fundamental misunderstandings that are leaving.

Not everyone will get there, we would say, in this lifetime to fully expressing that breathing, living sense "I am" that does not have that duality and separateness with God. It is difficult in your planes of existence that are dualistic in nature. And because of the centuries of history of believing God is other, there's a lot to get through here, like a salmon upstream. It's possible, but there's a lot to get through here, a lot of layers of misperception—sometimes intentional, sometimes not—that had been imposed upon humankind. This disbelief that "I am God," that "I am the all-that-is." It is one of the things that is leaving, and not everyone will get all of the way in this lifetime. But if you were to look from when you were a child to when you eventually exit this Earth and look back on humankind and the ability to perceive your own light, it will be vastly, vastly different by then, by the time you exit.

# THE BLISS OF THE ALL

## ANGEL ARIEL

We take you now into the silence of your own being. The place beyond wishing. Before you were creator being, before you were created, you were in this silent knowing of what we would call God, of what you might call vibration, awareness, consciousness. Before it became the bliss of becoming, you were in the bliss of knowing, in the bliss of the all. Before you delighted in the many, many colorful aspects of your unique being, you were in the beautiful void or rainbow of all.

Anytime it feels like this wishing, this becoming, is too much work, too much dizziness, we invite you to come back to the center, to the silent point of what you are, into the all-that-is.

It is not a paradox that you are both. You are an expression of divinity, and you are also <u>all</u> of divinity. You are the all-that-is.

Do not limit yourself to those expressions of the mind, beliefs of what you thought you were. When you are the all-that-is in this great dance, you can become anything you like, for as long as, or as short as, it is delightful to you to dance in that manner.

You are the creator of your world and you are also your world. It is created, in that sense, within the womb of you. You are this entire creation of yourself. This entire becoming.

# PART V
# EMBODIMENT OF CHANGE

# THE CHOICE BETWEEN THIRD AND FIFTH DIMENSIONS

## ANGEL RAPHAEL

It is free choice now. Each being (animal, human) on this planet (and there are other types of beings, but for now, we will stay today with the topic of animals and humans)—each being has a choice now that what we will call for shorthand fifth dimension has arrived: to be in this new way of being, fifth dimension, or to be in third, or to stay in both for a little while.

For some of you, part of the strong physical symptoms are the jumping back and forth now, between third and fifth, because you are a way shower for others. Energetically by crossing over to fifth dimension, those around you and even those not physically around you, can "see" on a psychic or a physical or energetic quantum level that you have crossed over. In seeing that it is like a mother doing something and the child watching and imitating, as a way shower as you jump over to fifth dimension and look backward to those still on third, they look towards you energetically and say: Oh, that's how it works. And then they themselves are able to cross over. So for some of you now you will be shuttling back and forth between third and fifth for a little while here.

So you have the choice now to stay in fifth all the time, to shuttle back and forth to show others, or to stay in third. You are allowed to change your mind in any moment.

It is not that consciously you need to say: Oh, okay, I'm going to go to fifth now. And then: Oh, I left someone behind, I'm going to go to third. This is happening quite naturally on a quantum level for you, because of your soul intention to help others (if you are the ones shuttling back and forth right now). So you do not need to understand conceptually with the mind how this works. It just is what is happening right now.

There will come a time in your lifetimes—not so far away from now, so not

even five years perhaps—where this easy ability to shuttle back and forth will no longer be there. The doors will close between this third dimension and fifth dimension. An easier way perhaps conceptually to experience this is like if there were a glacier ice shelf, a flat ice shelf, and it has split apart. There is to crack there—small crack. It is easy now to step back and forth over the two planes. But as they drift wider and wider apart, fewer and fewer will make that journey. And then at some point they are so far apart, they don't even see each other. So the idea of going back and forth doesn't arise in consciousness.

Of course, there will always be those who can travel between the different dimensions just a there are those who can travel to different planets and planes of existence now and have been able to for their whole lifetime.

So you understand when we say the doors are closed, it does not mean for everyone for all time. But that you will have drifted so far apart, it does not occur to those on third to think of fifth anymore. It does not occur to those on fifth to think back to third. So this is a time of choosing. It is a time, in a way, of great upheaval, but only upheaval because it feels so new. Not upheaval because things are wrong or going down the toilet. They might feel that way physically. We want to affirm again and again for you this is not the case. You are not making this up—the physical symptoms are quite strong, the emotional upheaval is quite strong. But it is because of landing from this voyage in quite a new plane of existence and adjusting to that.

∾

*Q: Is there a way to tell if you're in the third or the fifth dimension?*

Third and fifth dimension operate quite differently. So in the fifth dimension, there is no time. So if you feel that you wish something or think something and it happens faster than is logically possible, that is a good sign that you are in fifth dimension. Another hallmark of fifth dimension is that spatial relationships are quite different. So you might feel this as spaciness, you might also feel it as a lack of boundaries—where before perhaps Russia felt so far away, it seems quite conceivable now to just hop on a plane and visit tomorrow. So if you have these very different feelings about time and space, you are likely at that moment in fifth dimension.

Third dimension will be more familiar to all of you. It functions more where things take a long time to occur. And it is more linear. So that is that idea that I should make a plan, make a list, strive for something and maybe in 40 years or one year I'll get there. That is more of a hallmark of third dimension.

Third dimension also has a stronger sense of identity. So when you are feeling—more for those of you going back and forth—so fully in your shell of identity and your own identity preferences, you're probably more in third. And when you have those moments where you're feeling quite connected with everyone and just dancing with different qualities and ways of being but not feeling so fixed in your own personality, that is more of a hallmark of fifth dimension.

Bliss, here in this case, in this time of transition, is not the way to tell. Meaning, if you are in bliss does not mean necessarily that you are in fifth and if you are in pain does not necessarily mean that you are in third because of the upheaval that the physical body is feeling just now in this temporary timeframe. So whether or not you are enjoying the experience is not the way to tell at this moment that you are in fifth. We say this because for many of you, you have learned that as you come closer to enlightenment, or as you move up the food chain of spiritual existence, you will be feeling lighter and lighter and have laughter and bliss. And in some senses, this is the case. But in this timeframe between fifth and third dimension, that is not the easiest way to tell where you are.

∼

*Q: If some of us choose to stay in third and some move on to fifth, how will we interact and problem solve and move forward as a common species if we are divided by this dimensional shift in the future?*

This is a beautiful question. It comes from a heart that wishes to include everyone in the upliftment of humanity. So we want you to know from angelic perspective that third is not a negative choice. What we mean is, third dimension has its own hallmarks and values. So, in third dimension, for example, it is a little easier to work things out through love relationships, through this linear one-on-one husband, wife, parent, child, all types of love relationships, even work relationships. So for those who still feel on a soul level there is something so strong to work out with this person or persons that they are in a lifetime with now, they might feel there is more value to staying in third dimension for the rest of this existence. So staying on third does not mean stopping evolution or spiraling downward. From our perspective, it is a choice of different ways of being, different ways of existing.

From those on fifth, yes, for a little while, you will not be able to relate any longer in this lifetime with those on third dimension. But you have experienced this before. You have experienced loved ones passing on, animals dying, and so forth. And you know that on a soul level, you will encounter those beings again if you wish it. So no one is ever lost to us. The separation of humanity into these two spheres—third and fifth—is a "real" separation, yet it is also temporary.

Let us take again the person who stayed on third dimension to work through these family love relationships. Then at the end of this lifetime, they are not limited to stay in third dimension. They might move up to 11th or move to some other galactic plane of existence. You are not limited, of course, to births here on the Earth plane, either plane, and you could switch back and forth in between lifetimes also. So third dimension and fifth dimension will both continue to exist, it looks like from how humanity is evolving. Yes, there will be the inability to travel back and forth once those doors are closed. But that does not mean that you are fixed and stuck in that dimension for the rest of all of your lifetimes of existence. And of course, there will be those who can travel back and forth energetically and galactically as well, even in this lifetime.

Fifth dimension and third dimension each have their different ways of being, different ways of learning. One of our main viewpoints here is: Are people learning or not learning? So it is not the kind of ethical judgments you might have learned in church, of what is bad and what is good. But we like to see: Are people learning what they wished to learn coming into this lifetime? And for some of you, you will want to stay in third dimension in order to live out those lessons and really get the *rasa*, the juice, of why you came here to Earth.

From angelic perspective, this is quite a neutral choosing. From let us say a "New Age" (just to give it a label) from a "spiritual" perspective, we understand there is this great pull to label fifth dimension as higher, as better. And that is not the case. Truly speaking, from our perspective, it is not the case. But for those of you who have chosen fifth dimension, it is a dimension with much more freedom. So rapid growth for you can occur here. So it is a very positive place to be. But it is not the only place to learn. And some people prefer to learn slower. So third dimension might be more suitable for that.

*Q: Is it related to the shifting of poles? The frequencies of the north and the south are said to be shifting—like the north will become the south, the south become the north? Can you speak on that?*

The earth has gone through most of the changes that she will undergo —most of the dramatic changes. So in the past—2017, 2018—you saw many, many weather events, volcanic events, hurricanes and so forth. This was the earth shifting quite severely—changing course into different winds, to use the metaphor of a sailboat. Things felt quite stormy there for a little while. Changes will still occur, yes, but from where this question is coming from—the question of the physical earth—most of those shifts have already occurred.

We do not expect more of that exact type of shifting, in the future days and months. What we do expect is that Earth yourself is coming alive, as a being. Some cultures already respect Earth as Goddess or something like this. And the earth in the past has been certainly an alive energy, but not what we would call an embodied, singular soul, the way it is waking up to be now. Some of you will have the opportunity in this lifetime to interact with Earth—and we do mean planet Earth here—as a physical being, as a soul (that is the closest word we can say to give the distinction here). Certainly there were sacred energies there before. And perhaps those cultures knew there was a dormancy there that would awaken one day. As you awaken into this fifth dimension, Earth also is awakening in fifth, as a soul, as a being that you will be able to interact with. As this being wakens, there will be a little more of the shifting you have experienced in 2017, 2018—earthquakes and so forth. But it will be from what we can see much more gentle. It is just that some shifts will still occur. Very like—metaphorically speaking—the child in the womb that is moving around creates a little rumbling, but then it is not disturbing for the mother, but certainly it is felt.

Like that, beings on Earth may begin to experience and feel—

energetically more than physically—that something is new and different with the quality of Earth. That will be something to experiment with energetically. For those of you who like to connect energetically with other beings, you might start speaking with Earth, if you like. She's a little mute just now. So if you tried today, you might not get much of a response. But you might be surprised at some near future that this arrives on the palate of beings you can interact with, along with your angels and guides and so forth. This Earth is a living being now.

∼

*Q: Will healing work the same in fifth dimension?*

Physical pains now, even physical illnesses, in fifth dimension are more of a hallmark, a signpost to say: pay attention here. In third dimension a physical pain, meant: run to the doctor, or exercise more, take a tincture, or get Reiki, or something like that. It wanted to be addressed on the physical plane. In fifth dimension, a symptom in the physical body is more of a signpost to say: here in the shoulder, there was a past lifetime where some wrong occurred. Can you look into this, and address this on a soul level with that other being please? Can you look into meditating with this physical circumstance (symptom) and see what feels right? See what feels necessary to move that energy in the energetic space. So healing will occur more and more. It has been subtle for many of you, things like Reiki or energy work have worked well. It will become even more so, where the healing that needs to take place—through shamanic work, through sound work, through Reiki, through meditation, through shifting, through acknowledging and facing the energies that are stored in the physical body for the time being--so that they can be released and relieved and moved on. Then you will find the physical symptom disappears once the core issue behind it is addressed.

∼

*Q: The decision whether to stay in a third of the fifth before the doors close—how will we know when that shows up?*

It is not one decision point. Many have seen this time and illustrated it as a glowing moment where it is so evident and obvious that the doors are open and you are walking through into a New World. Then here you are on violet clouds with angels or something else visibly very different.

In fact, if you are reading these words, you have already walked through that gateway to fifth dimension more than once. You have already experienced this back and forth and what it feels like—some days you are in that experience of collapsed time where you think something and it happens immediately; where the synchronicities, if you like, are so powerful that you are just in the flow . . . walking out to the mailbox at the very moment the postman drives up or it might be larger events . . . but the synchronicities and collapsed time might be felt in very small ways also. So feeling very, very much in the flow of existence and attuned to and one with what is happening. When you are feeling more like struggling against the world, or alone, or otherwise separate and distinct—that is a more third-dimensional hallmark.

It is not that there is a test that must be passed, or that you must say out loud: "Okay, I choose fifth dimension." Or: "Okay, I choose third." Energetically on a soul level, you have made this choice a long time ago. So your energetic being is moving according to your wishes as they were stated before you came into this lifetime. That does not mean that you are locked in. We will say many times: you have free choice. Even though you have made that choice to be in the fifth dimension, and to start that transition now, you still have free choice to change your mind at any moment. And some who are on third dimension and not enjoying the experience of the cacophony of distraction right now will choose to leave the planet entirely. So you might see more people exiting at this time. Understand that it is choice, it does not mean we are in a time where we are failing as a species or anything like that. The choice often happens on the soul level before we enter a lifetime.

Those of you who came into this lifetime at this time on Earth, you really came for this experience—for this newness, for this shift to another dimensional reality. That said, even if you bought a plane ticket to Spain, if when you arrived you didn't like it, you can still get on a boat or a train to Portugal—go somewhere else. So, if you find that you change your mind for whatever reason, you may change the course of your own destiny. That is more available to you now on Earth as a human than it has ever been before. You are no longer being dictated to about the course of your evolution. You are free. You are free to choose again.

That said, this entry point into the fifth dimension could happen very subtly, can happen in your sleep, in meditation. It has happened for all of you already at least once. So it is quite subtle in a way. It is not so obvious when you are walking back and forth. It is just that, as the question earlier brought out—How can I tell if I'm in third or fifth?—there are some hallmarks you'll begin to see where you are in any given moment. Then you could choose in that moment consciously: "Oh, this feels a lot like third and it feels uncomfortable. Is my body all right with going back to fifth now? Because I like it better there."

You could experiment with this quite playfully, although it is a huge and massive change for humanity, and so it is presented as such by those who are channels, guides, teachers, meditators. That is true. And at the same time, it does not have to be so serious and so final. It is not like that. You may play with this, dance back and forth. See if you can consciously move to the different dimensions. That is a little more difficult just now. It will become easier, but for some of you it is possible already. But certainly by stating your intention, the energy will move in your system when it is able.

∽

*Q: How does the fourth dimension play in what is going on here with the shifting?*

Fourth dimension in an energetic space is the place of the heart. It is why many teachers speak now of speaking from the heart, deciding from the heart, dropping into your heart, meditating at a doorway in your heart, you will hear this again and again. Fourth has access to both third and fifth, although it is not necessary to cross through fourth to get to fifth. It is the easiest place to be in this moment where we are dancing between third and fifth dimensions.

The heart is quite comfortable with both—third and fifth. So if you are feeling uncomfortable, physically or otherwise, why not drop into the space of the heart? However that works for you energetically; there is no magic formula. Many people, guides, have some very sweet ways of doing this. But all it really requires is your intention to move to the place of the heart. Then from that place, experience what is happening and also issue your own commands about what you wish to happen for your own life existence here. When we say command, we don't mean the commanding <u>over</u> anyone else—taking anyone else's sovereignty—but commanding your own space of freedom. Understanding that you are free to have your wishes be known—we call this a command—in the heart space, and that can play out in third or fifth. It is also more comfortable a place to weather a lot of these changes.

∼

*Q: What does the sixth dimension represent?*

This is a beautiful question to open more generally the idea of dimensional realities, because conceptually it is something that is a little new for most of us. What does this really mean? Does a higher dimension mean you are closer (higher) to enlightenment? It does not. Traveling to other planes of existence, it would be very similar to traveling to a different planet, or any other universe where the rules of gravity and other laws of existence are different: different food sources, different types of water, and so forth. On a very practical level, dimensional awareness, dimensional being, you can think of it—although this is not exactly accurate—as a different place you are visiting. It is closer to what is true reality here than to think of it as moving higher towards enlightenment. Although in this case, the change on Earth also brings many people closer to that. That is a together with; it's not because of.

Sixth dimension is another quality of being. There are other types of physical beings, although you will not see them on Earth, who exist in sixth dimension. They have different hallmarks and qualities of being. Let us pause for a moment to go more generally.

There is some confusion here as people seek their "true" identity, where they look to see: Am I a star seed? Am I an Andromedan? Am I Lemurian? Am I angel? Am I human? It can cause quite a lot of identity confusion. Understand that this is not a linear happening, but we will present it as such so that the mind can understand. In some lifetime, let us say you were angel. And then in another lifetime, you came to Earth and you were Lemurian. And then in the next lifetime, you spent some time in the Pleiades. And then in the next lifetime, you are human on Earth. And then the next lifetime you are human on Earth, but you were confused: Am I angel? Am I Andromedan? Am I Lemurian? Am I Pleiadian? And you look to others for these answers.

You are what you are in this exact moment. This is complete freedom. You are not chained to being an angel. You are not chained to being an Andromedan. You are not chained to being a sixth-dimensional being. Right now, you are here on Earth at this choice point, all of you, between third and fifth dimension. A year, ten years, one lifetime from now, you will have other choices: to become angel again, to decide whether or not to be human on fifth dimension...

The core identity here is God, is source energy, is the all-that-is. We are part of the same light. You are not so different from angel or sixth-dimensional being, or third dimensional being or fifth dimensional being. In this exact moment you have complete freedom from all of these identifications.

Enlightenment, from our perspective, is understanding that you are already free. Having the ability in each moment to move through any of these dimensional places, ways of being, ways of interacting with others. Understanding that you are this purest form of light—and forgive our language it is difficult to fully express what we mean, so we call it light. What we mean is this type of freedom that is so completely vast, so completely unlimited. And that is what you are in this moment, and each moment truly. Although we spoke at length about what is happening on your planet, to your physical body, it is also true that in this exact moment, you are completely free of all of that. You are completely free of all of these identifications and ways of being. You can move throughout all layers of dimensional existence freely.

# PHYSICAL ADAPTATIONS

## ANGEL RAPHAEL

There is a physical adaptation happening. We spoke about moving from third to fifth dimension. This is aligned with but separate from this freedom from subjugation. So it is a physical thing. It is a movement from third dimension, which you're quite familiar with, so we don't have to give all the hallmarks. But one of them is linear thinking; one of them is time; another is money. The denser, harder ways of forcing through things. It's that story you see played in so many movies where the odds are stacked against you, but you're hoping you are going to be the one to break free—to be wealthy or be the football player against all odds, or whatever it is. That's the hallmark of third dimension. It seems like everything is stacked against you. And it's very hard. But there is some possibility there, so you strive to break out that way. That is the third-dimensional way of being. You're quite practiced at that. So when you have a goal that you're trying to reach, right away you go into that mode of: here's the list of things I'll need to accomplish, here is the amount of time it's going to take, here are the resources I might need—money or whatever it is, degree, pedigree, the right friends, and so on. That's the old way of getting there.

In the fifth dimension it is much more as we described this daydreaming and looking into the wide-open sky. That's the closest metaphor we have here for being in a place of total relaxation and almost whimsical wishing. "What if I could have this?" It doesn't come with a sense of struggle—the sense of: "all right, here we go. It's going to be a long journey. But I'm going to make it. I'm going to be one to break free here, and get what I want, get to the top of the mountain."

The fifth-dimensional way of calling things in is much more like building castles in clouds. It feels very fanciful at first. But it's that easy. You are just imagining what you might like to wish for. And once you decide on that, it's just being clear with your heart and with your angels: "This is what I want. This is what I'd like to try." And you're not locked in the way you would have been in third dimension to only one wish or three or seven wishes in this lifetime. You can be very playful with continually changing your wishes. So it feels a little frivolous to the third-dimensional mind. The wishes don't all need to be serious. And they don't need to be based in time or reliant on money. It's very, very gentle, soft that way.

To go back to this question: Why does sometimes it feel like this dreamy, easy, easy way of being? And why does it sometimes feel like that old way where I'm carrying 40 pounds up the mountain? The new layer of this for us to describe here is the physical change from third to fifth dimension is not an instant one. Very, very similar—so similar that there's almost no distinction here—if the physical body were going to climb Everest, or some high mountain, there are certain protocols that are needed. The physical body needs to get used to the different levels of oxygen, the different levels of cold. So that's why there are these stages. The body needs to wait and adapt before it can climb higher.

Very, very similarly, your physical body is getting in readiness to live in fifth dimension all of time. But for now what you are getting is glimpses of it. Maybe a few hours or a day where you're there in fifth dimension, where things suddenly just arrive at your doorstep.

They're so easy, so delightful. And then you feel you go crashing back into the reality you had known which now feels even slower, more sluggish and more painful by contrast.

Understand that it's not that you keep almost getting there and missing the boat, as if you are needing to leap over a chasm. It's a physical adaptation. So it's going to feel like this up down, up down for a little while. Where you sometimes are aware you are in more fifth-dimensional reality, and sometimes more in third. It's not a linear progress from one to the other. It's an acclimation, a physical acclimation, to being there all the time. So the good news is you will get there. The bad news is, despite the fact that you can taste in some hours, some days how instant reality is, within the construct of the body, which is mostly in linear third-dimensional time right now, it's not instant to get there. So you can see it, you can experience it. And it's not a linear journey to get there.

So again, you don't have to have a plan and struggle to get there. But understand, it's going to take some time. And there are going to be pockets of what feels like density, particularly for the physical body and the emotional body, as the body acclimates, and gets used to this higher dimension.

Being in fifth dimension and being enlightened is not the same thing. Moving to fifth dimension has all these hallmarks we've talked about —that instant way of melting into the realities you want and receiving them. But it's also a very physical state of being; so you're making a transition there. And it doesn't mean once you get there, you're enlightened. But you might be more inclined to continue to drop old structures within your brain space, for example, to jump more quickly to enlightenment. Having witnessed within your own lifetime what would seem quite impossible—the migration of the human race from one dimension to another—you might start believing that many things are possible, including your own enlightenment. But it is a separate thing—the shift from one dimension to another.

One of the reasons why we speak about the distinction between ascension to fifth dimension and ascension in an enlightenment sense is for those of you who are used to tuning into higher energies through meditation or other ways are used to that those beautiful, subtle, uplifting feelings and you associate that with enlightenment.

Then when you come into a period, as we're coming in to now, in this time on Earth in the next year or so very broadly, generally speaking, where it's so much about physical adaptation, you might begin to doubt yourself. "Did I fall off of the enlightenment path? Because I used to feel so subtle and light in that sense, and what I feel now is brain fog or weight gain or these physical, unpleasant symptoms. And what does this have to do with anything? I must have started eating the wrong thing or thinking the wrong thing, or what the heck is happening here?"

It is in this year or so a very, very physical time of adaptation and not necessarily a comfortable one. There's no risk there. From our perspective, angelic perspective, the bodies are going to make it through this. But there's a reason why it's a slow process, because the body doesn't want to be jarred into instantaneously living on fifth or higher, different dimensions. Just understand if there's confusion there that: "Wait a minute. I'm being told now also from others that humanity is in this unprecedented time. Why do I feel worse? I used to be able to meditate so much easier two years ago. And now I'm just sort of obsessed with how difficult the body is."

There are a few different answers to this. One is just be compassionate; give your body the attention it needs through this. It's intelligent enough to make the transition. You don't need to intellectually know how to support it. But there are some obvious things. When you feel that tired, please rest. Or when you feel such brain fog, are you trying to push through third-dimensional activities? Maybe you have enough flexibility in your schedule that you don't have to do that just then. Maybe in that moment, when you're feeling brain fog, you're actually quite attuned to fifth and you could to drop into meditation, or even to sit and daydream about your life moving forward—if you're feeling physically unwell, and meditation isn't attractive, for example.

There's two ways of approaching this. One is be compassionate; the body is going through quite a lot. And don't expect it to rush there. You're not doing anything wrong. The second is, if you're going to continue to try to do fifth-dimensional instantaneous kind of thinking while you're in third, you're going to feel a little frustrated in those moments. Similarly, if you're going to continue to try to push through third-dimensional activities when you're in fifth, it's going to feel very . . .brain fog, we would say is most likely that kind of symptom, when you're lifted up for those few hours at a time into a more fifth-dimensional ease of being and you're trying to force through something that's very linear at that time, it doesn't make sense. It's almost like if you were in a three-dimensional movie trying to walk in a two-dimensional way. It's a dimensional mismatch. That's why it feels disorienting in a physical way.

We understand there could be some frustration. You'd like to either be in one or the other and learn the rules of the game and just proceed forward. But out of compassion and necessity for the body taking some time to make this journey, it will be back and forth for some time here. The best way we would say is: When you're in water, swim; and when you're in the air, fly. When it feels very boring, dense, heavy, get your computer work done. When it feels that you were so ethereal that you can barely believe you have a body, meditate or do some dreaming about how you'd like your life to be.

Be in the time that you're in. You're not in most cases going be able to control the timing of it. But you can adjust to it. And that can feel more and more easeful as you just surrender, in a sense, to what is. "Okay. I'm back on third. Did I have some laundry to do? We'll have some magical, sparkly time in a few hours."

## ASCENDING IN THE PHYSICAL BODY

### ANGEL ARIEL

*Q: Is it possible for us to ascend and remain in physical form?*

Yes, many have done so. In your lifetime there have been some--not so publicized. But certainly in the course of humanity, there are some that many of you can think of who have ascended and stayed as a physical being. We can mention Buddha because that seems like an undisputed answer for tonight for the people here.

Yes, one can ascend in a human physical body and stay in the physical body. It is easier at the moment of death for ascension to occur, and that's why often it happens then, as opposed to in the physical body. But certainly, yes, it is possible to hold ascension energy in the physical body. And you will find in your lifetimes now moving forward, in the next 20 years or so, many, many people will make this choice. There is an acceleration there also. Whereas before maybe once every thousand years, there were the exceptions, there were beings who took embodiment and ascension at the same time. Now we have a situation where as humanity accelerates many, many beings will make that choice. And you may or may not know. It might be your brother or your friend, and you might not know. It might not be so evident from the outside, because the physical body—the habits, taste preferences might be the same.

But we would say generally this is becoming so accessible to humankind, that we will be surprised if it does not become an epidemic [laughing] of embodied enlightened masters. Perhaps these will not all be teachers, but ascended energies, yes.

It becomes much, much more accessible now, because now that you can wish for something it's not just houses and cars and new jobs and new family members you can wish for—new life circumstances. For ascension to happen in your energy—to know who you are—is also available to you now. And again time and money have been removed as obstacles in the equation, so you have many people arising very quickly once they make that clear decision: This is what I want. So it need not be such a path of suffering as it was for those that are historical examples of that. So many years in the forest. It will be a different time now.

∼

*Q: I've heard it said that we need to some extent go through the pain in order to heal. Is that still true?*

If a knife were being removed from the physical body, then pain is required as it exits. But could that process be instantaneous? So fast that the perception of pain was almost infinitesimal? Yes. Similarly, what you might call "pain" has to do with from our perspective, the shiftings of energy—the choice to move an energy out in order to bring in more light or more peace or some other quality that you want. You feel that viscerally, the way when you move from a hot space to cold space, you feel the change. What you call pain, we would say is this shifting of awareness of the fact that energy is shifting. In that sense yes, we do see it as one of the natural ingredients of change, of bringing in more light. But it can happen so fast, now. Where it doesn't have to be 20 years of being aware that your heart is healing. It could be two minutes or so. So yes, but it could be much, much more rapid now.

∼

*Q: It feels like my spiritual progress has slowed down.*

As you are looking at your changing landscape, you have a few options here. There are changes within your own self, your own being —meaning how you see the world, or how you mature in different ways, spiritually speaking. Physical things. We want you to feel a little compassionate on yourself that you don't have to change everything in the same moment. It is enough that the whole world is changing around you. You don't also—in this year, these two years when change is so rapid and complete—you don't also have to have that pressure on yourself of becoming enlightened or transforming from within at the exact same time that everything is changing. It's enough to have one or the other. You have spent quite a lot of focus on the interior transformation. And so that habit is there. But understand that if you are attempting to continue to grow internally at the same pace that you have been in this lifetime, at the same time as the whole world around you—all of the social structures, all of the energetic ways of being, your physical body—all of this is changing at the same time; it could feel like too much (on some days, particularly).

So please be compassionate with yourself. We understand how the perception might be: "This is my time window to fly into enlightenment. It's now or never. Things are wide open. Now is the time for the change." We want you to know things are wide open, but they're not going to close again. So it's not a limited opportunity here. And it is a lot for the physical vessel, especially right now, to take on the changes that are going on. So please be compassionate with yourself. If you feel like: Why am I not <u>also</u> having the huge spiritual growth moments (or perceiving it that way) at the same time as the whole planet, and my body, and all of my relationships are changing? Perhaps, that's a little much to expect of yourself.

We understand the beauty of the intention where that comes from. But we want you to know this is not a lost moment, if all of the transformation doesn't happen at once. Things will remain wide open. And in some cases, if you're choosing, for example—let's put this in a kind of a stark example, a little more than is the truth just for an example here . . . If you're choosing between calibrating your space suit to the New Earth, or having an inner space change, enlightenment kind of change, and you choose the inner space change, and your space suit isn't recalibrated, well then the physical vessel dies, and you have to start over again or continue in the in-between spaces [between lifetimes]. Of course, we don't believe that you die with your body. Again, we overstated that a little. But we want you to know that the physical changes are quite important right now, for the very practical reason of just adapting to the new world and surviving here. It's a very, very practical level like that. Even though from a spiritual vantage point it doesn't feel so lofty sometimes. It doesn't feel as exciting, sometimes, to be focusing so much on the tiredness or the changes in the physical vessel. It is important. It is an essential ingredient to being able to stick around and enjoy these energetic times.

We do promise there will be times for enlightenment also, for all of those inner journeys. But this time, this moment on Earth, is more about the physical. You are not sacrificing your enlightenment by just being here and absorbing the changes.

It's okay to just be in more of a receptive mode. There's so much going on right now. By allowing that, by being a little patient with that, then you have so many more decades to play with these new energies. So that's your choice. Of course, you could choose to leave all that behind and just take the fast track to enlightenment and leave the body also. That's also a choice. There's nothing wrong about doing it that way.

Why do things seem to be slowing down in a sense, just when

everything energetically is speeding up? It's not an accident. It's that your capacity to grow and change is being more directed toward the physical right now. It has nothing to do with the fact that you are becoming less spiritual or that this year you are less good at those things. That from our vantage point would be a misperception of what's happening.

# SHEDDING HEAVY LAYERS

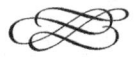

## ANGEL ARIEL AND ANGEL RAPHAEL

*Angel Ariel:*

There is a great disillusionment happening on your planes of existence. (There are more than one now, planes of existence). There is a great disillusionment happening. As this occurs, as you come closer to knowing who you are, and how things really work in this universe of light, of which you are the core, the center. . . as this disillusionment is occurring, it is a little bit like a winter coat being dropped onto the floor, or the puss of a boil coming out; it seems much more visible. If you were wearing the coat, you're not so aware; but when you take it off, you see it, you feel the weight of it. Same of course, anything leaving the skin or the physical systems of the body —as they exit, you're much, much more aware. And then you think something must be wrong. But it is actually in that moment when things are being expelled from you.

So in this phase we are in on these planes of existence, what is happening with humankind is you are losing, shedding, some of these disillusionments. As they are shedding, the heaviness of them is more apparent. That's why we use this analogy of the winter coat. You're holding this thing, or watching it drop, and you are just looking at the ugliness, the heaviness, the weightiness of it, because now it's spring and you don't need such a thing. It feels too hot, and very, very uncomfortable.

Be aware that many of you are feeling that you have somehow backslid, or that things have gotten dark on the planet. It is not so. And yet we want to verify your own feeling and understanding. Your perception in this is correct. You are perceiving the heaviness and that is correct. But what we want you to know is that it is leaving and that is why it is more apparent now. It is a little bit of a paradox for the mind to understand. But it is something that is leaving. It is not something that is being imposed upon you. It is not a brain chemistry mishap or other reason why the heaviness feels stronger now.

It is a time of change. When the human physical system perceives change, it goes into a sort of red alert, which is humorous since change is always ongoing here. But still, your systems now perceiving change are heightened. They are looking around for what the threat is to the physical existence, because a change is here. What is the new predator animal in the forest that I need to be aware of? It is that kind of level of a red alert that we mean. Fight or flight kind of mechanisms get alerted here.

So you have this heightened sense of danger, just because change is here. And you layer on to this, this experience of the heaviness leaving you, and then the mind comes in to interpret. "Aha! it must be that there's a particular heaviness now, and my system is alerting me it's dangerous, and so I better quickly figure out what it is. Things must have gone wrong in this planetary experiment. I thought things were going really well." (This is the voice of the mind, now—Ariel speaking about the mind.) "I thought things were going very well, but now they feel very heavy. So I better spend a lot of time spinning my mental wheels, figuring out what went wrong and fix it fast 'cause this is very uncomfortable."

Hopefully this feels familiar for you; you can resonate with this. If it is familiar, it is easier then to discard and laugh about what is happening here. All of your beautiful functioning human systems are trying to solve a problem that does not exist. They have been alerted to change, they feel the extra heaviness which is leaving, and the mind, the physical systems are all scrambling around dancing, trying to save you.

We want to add a different perspective, a different lens of perception here, which is in fact this heaviness is leaving—is leaving you personally, is also leaving collectively the human consciousness. And when this is done leaving, this layer of disillusionment, you will begin to see deeper layers of light within yourself. In these times of doubt, in these times of extra heaviness in the perception, you can come again to this remembrance of the light within yourself, even if some days the heaviness is so strong that it's just a mental concept. Then at least in those moments, the mind has something else to think about other than: whatever is wrong, I better fix it fast.

For your highest good and direction of where you're going you do not want to alleviate this heaviness just now. It's leaving you. So to alleviate it means stuff it back down, pretend it's not there, stop the process of this great disgorgement, this great disillusionment that is happening. Because you will see also as you perceive this greater heaviness, you are perhaps also perceiving great flashes of insight, of understanding about the world around you in ways that are quite sharp and sudden.

These are the gifts that come as the heaviness leaves. Then the ease of perception is what takes its place. That in itself is another layer which might be a little jarring—getting used to the heightened perception and understandings you will have now. And the abilities to communicate with other beings. Telepathy understanding also is quite heightened now. So it's an interesting mix of flashes of truth, flashes of understanding, and then this great heaviness. We want you to know that in this short period of time, perhaps there is nothing you can do to alleviate this feeling of heaviness. That from our perspective in a sense is also good, because you do not want to stop the shedding of the winter coat, the shedding of the misperceptions.

How do you have an easier road in the meantime? You can tell your mind this story, which from our perspective is also true, that you are light. And you can move into that sensation, shift your awareness a little bit from the shells that are leaving towards the inner light. And you should be able to find some relief there in the lighter places which are a little more core within you.

In a more global sense, many of you are feeling physically heavier. Sometimes [this] might be physical weight, but also could be the manifestation of old injuries like arthritis-type feelings—you're not quite sure where they're coming from, they're not quite acute enough, perhaps to seek medical attention, or maybe the doctors aren't finding anything there... That kind of general dis-ease and heaviness in the body is quite common now. It is part of the same transmission of energies outward and away from you, let us say.

It is an interesting mystery here that as heaviness, let's say whatever is the opposite of light—even though the whole universe is made up of light, so we bring in paradox along with mystery here—let's say there was something called the opposite of light, and it was called heaviness, and it was leaving from this core of you outward. It is expressing itself as it leaves for some in the emotional systems—a heaviness like depression. And for some in the physical system, heaviness like extra weight gain or pains in the body. All of these are positive expressions at this time that the absence of light, this heaviness, is moving farther and farther away from your core, your center, which is light. This is a temporary condition, we would say generally for those of you who have been experiencing dull aches and things that don't quite make sense in a medical sense; this heaviness, this dis-ease in the body, it is leaving. You will come into a time of greater light there.

It does require perhaps patience, the patience of the ant to carry such heavy loads and know that you are capable of that. And also that there will be an end point to this suffering of heaviness—that it is in fact at its height right now, which is why it comes up as a topic. So now when it feels at its worst, the heaviness is in fact getting the farthest from you. So it is nearly done. It is nearly done. So please take comfort that this is a positive change, and a temporary one.

∾

*Q: Is there a way to best support our bodies through these changes?*

Although you have asked about the body, the most direct answer is that the mind needs to know that it's all right, that the body doesn't need urgent fixing. Because it has felt very much like something needs urgent attention, mental health attention or physical attention—that it must really, really be time and urgently to address things on a physical level. We want the mind to know this is not the case. We understand why it is perceived that way. And please tell your minds they are doing a great job of looking out for you. Just because things are new, they haven't quite learned to see what's really happening here. What is happening is that this density, this heaviness emotionally and physically speaking, is leaving. Collectively, humans are going to become lighter.

There are some bands of disillusionment, some bands of density, which are from our perspective a very physical reality, but are sometimes expressed in more metaphysical ways. However it is that you perceive it, if it is very physical—we think for most of you has been very physical or emotional expression of late—then maybe take comfort in the fact that it is a physical expression. But it is a metaphysical one as well. It is the leaving of some density here. So there is nothing that you need to fix for the most part. Of course, there will always be cases when some on the planet right now are physically experiencing heart attacks or other things that need direct physical intervention. But for the most part, for those of you reading this now, we want you to know this physical and emotional heaviness is not a crisis that needs a physical intervention, although it feels that way.

It needs a mental intervention, to have the patience to know—to have the serenity through this—that it is leaving you. And it is a temporary discomfort, no matter how strong it might be. This discomfort is temporary. You are right in perceiving it. It is real. And yet it is not something in you that needs to be fixed. The very heightened nature of its expression means it is leaving you. It is leaving you.

~

*Q: How long will this last?*

This is Raphael. So we can say with some certainty that this will not last. It is a great and extraordinary upheaval outward, the way a volcanic explosion is just pushing molten earth out through the crust. So it can't go on forever. There is not a bottomless pit of things to discharge here. This particular layer, although it seems very dramatic, is quite light. Because it is of the denser physical and emotional misperceptions/realities here. That layer from our perspective is quite shallow. It doesn't have much weight in a metaphysical sense. It doesn't have much reality to it. Because of that, it leaves more quickly. You feel it perhaps more concretely in the physical parts of the being, emotional and physical parts of the being. But it is not a heavy layer, it is quite a shallow layer.

Forgive us if we bring confusion with using different metaphors, because we spoke of it as heaviness. What we mean is if you were to shift now to this metaphor of crusts of earth, from the core outward, this crust layer is very, very fragile, brittle, and it will discharge quite quickly here. The more in a sense that it feels it is heightened, it is too much to bear, the more we would say it has left you already. It is almost nearly done.

There will be, from our perspective, more layers and shifting layers of this. So when you ask the question in this moment, the answer could be about two weeks for this current physical layer. And then you feel some waves of other changes, perhaps dizziness and lightheadedness, from so much light by contrast, and you feel: "Oh, thank goodness, this is done. There's no more heaviness for me." And then a few months later, you hit something that feels like a wall. It is quite dense again. So in this time, these few years roughly, there are many of these layers to be shed. Some of them have to do with density of the physical and emotional being. Some of them have to do with coming into light and adjusting to that lightness of being.

∼

*Q: Is this a good time to shed things in my life – job, mortgage, anything that feels like a burden right now? Or should I lie low and see if it passes?*

This is Ariel. Both are true. Meaning, if you were to not act on these impulses to shed the physical weight of responsibilities or sameness in job or physical possessions, or contracts to physical possessions, such as mortgages and leases and so on, if you were not to act on those urges, the heaviness that you feel from them will lighten over time just because you are moving more and more into these layers of lightness of being.

This is Raphael. Both are true, because there also is a very concrete heaviness to physical objects, to contracts we have with people and situations that when we let go of them, we do feel that weight is lifted. So, both are true. It is not necessary for you to change your job or your mortgage in order to come to this lightness of being. However, it is not a false lead.

It is part of, organically part of, this light seeking itself—this very, very primal impulse towards light. As a human (as a living conscious creature, so this is not limited to humans) the impulse towards light is the most organic, simple and freeing impulse. It is not necessary to take action in the physical world to bring about more light. Yet there is a correct perception here that possessions, circumstances if they have gone on for too long, do carry a heaviness which can be physically moved.

*Q: For the ascension process, how many layers of density are yet to lift?*

*Angel Ariel:*

Like the layers of Earth—we will go back to this metaphor of the crusts and layers of earth—like this, there are similarities in the stages of ascension process, but if you were to go to Alaska versus Venezuela, you will see different specific layers in the earth to be broken through. So each individual being also carries a variety of layers that are unique.

For you, the ascension process will look different than for husband, neighbor, friend, and so on. For each there is a similarity. If you look again to the earth, that molten core or a certain lead layer, or certain fossil layers, are similar anywhere you go on Earth. But then as you look closer and closer, those layers of moss, and debris and light and crystals are very, very specific and unique to each place on Earth.

Like that, each being has a different ascension path. There is more than one pathway even for one being. For example, if you were to meditate for 20 years, that might take you a certain distance, but also just as we had spoken of being in the proximity of someone who had turned toward their own light might get you there in an instant, where you had gone 20 years of meditation yourself, and these things are cumulative. So it is not one linear path. You take surges upward (to use a metaphor here for it is not literally "up" if it is anything it is more literally "in" but is generally spoken of as ascension, as moving up, so we will use the metaphoric language). As you move upward, it is cumulative. There are things that break through different layers and surge you upward and towards your truth, towards your being-less-ness and away—meaning shedding all of these false layers of believing your individual self and coming back into the wholeness, the purity of light that we all share.

So, it is not an easy answer in terms of time, because it is different for each being, depending on the actions you take. And here is where the free will and the individual path comes in. The choices you make individually towards meditation, towards being around others who are pointing into their own light for example, and there are many, many other pathways of intellectual knowledge, of metaphysical practices such as sacred geometry, holding crystalline friends, and so on. (We see crystals as conscious beings.) So interacting with other conscious beings, whether they are human or otherwise, also affects our ascension pathways. So your actions, although you are already—here is the paradox that has been oft stated but is true enough to say again now—although you are already God, you are already light, your actions towards this ascension process are what get you there to understanding, to knowing what is true there, what is already true.

Your actions are not necessary to create God within you, because God is already within you. But your actions are necessary for the understanding to dawn in you that this is the case. It is a very, very individual journey. At the same time, like those crusts of earth there are certain pathways, certain things that are known about the ascension process in humans more generally, which is why you can seek out the help of courses and teachers and they will have some truth for you. Typically, not all of one course or what one teacher has to say will resonate, will work for you. But there are often some very general truths that are helpful there. And then your own free will in acting upon them—for example, taking time to meditate, or taking time to shift your awareness towards your own light. Acting on those pieces of wisdom, of insight, are where you interact with your ascension pathway.

# TELEPATHY

## ANGEL ARIEL

*A*s the layers come thinner and we become more aware of who we are more directly, it becomes less of a fixed concept that: "I am so separate from that dog over there, that human over there, that shell over there" (the living shell not fossil). Those abilities, those pathways into telepathy—you are less tentative to approach them as you begin to conceptually and viscerally understand your oneness with everything here. Of course, to use a silly example, you know how to talk to yourself out loud. So if the shell and the dog and the other human are all yourself, of course you can talk to yourself. That's a silly way of expressing it, but it is true like that. As you become more and more aware of your direct connection to source, to God, to angelic light, however you like to phrase that (and please use the words that work for you, and don't feel that even angels should impose new words, if they feel foreign and misfit for you). So however you like to express that, to language it, as you become more and more in touch with being God, of course God knows how to speak to all the layers of its own being.

Like that, telepathy is a very practical simple tool, like tying your shoes or learning to walk or talk. It gets easier with practice, but it is an innate skill that is quite easy to use. The biggest barrier in these last lifetimes against telepathy has been the belief in separateness itself, not the fact that telepathy is so hard to learn and understand. If you approach it more innocently like that, if you begin to listen to the birds and angels and animals around you, you might be surprised that in fact you do understand their language. You just were not aware of it before because the mind had put up that layer, that shell that said: "I am separate." And that is not from our perspective, the truth. You are, in fact, quite un-separate from all of these people and other living creatures in your awareness.

It's time to start communicating with each other because there are delightful stories to share with each other, and because this is not an alone place. Part of the heaviness that is leaving now is this misogyny (and we use this word not to be gender specific, but because it is well understood right now), this misogyny of feeling alone when in fact we are not separate from all of these other beautiful creatures around us. Telepathy is just a simple and beautiful way out of this isolation and false aloneness that we have been feeling in human consciousness for some time. It is one of the greatest fallacies to be left here, to be left behind, shed as it were, this feeling: "I am alone." It is what is expressing in a very fundamental sense now through the emotional system, through the physical system.

"I am alone" is a false message. It is a false understanding. It must leave in order for this greater lightness of being, interconnectedness and enlightenment for some, but certainly movement towards enlightenment for all. Enlightenment as we are expressing it now being that complete understanding of who and what you are, and how you are not separate in any sense. As that leaves, as layers of that leave, it is expressing itself loudly right now. It is crying out to you: "I am alone, I am separate. I'm a dense physical being. And I'm in emotional pain and physical pain." This is the lie that is leaving. So understand it for what it is. You do not need to fix this by going out and having a party with friends are proving to yourself that you are not alone. There is no harm in doing so. But the core of what fixes this is allowing this dense layer of "I am alone, I am a dense, painful physical emotional being" to leave here. As we have said it is perceived as a heavy layer, a painful layer. But it is in fact quite a thin, brittle layer. It will leave quickly. There's nothing you need to do to push it out.

In our compassion, we want you to know it is a temporary thing. It is not something to be worried over from a mental perspective. You will not get there faster by believing you are in peril here. Nor will the misunderstanding that this is a danger keep you from getting towards this greater light that is happening. It is just a more uncomfortable layer. But it is only that. It is only a layer. And it is leaving. It is leaving.

## YOU ARE OPENING DOORWAYS

### ANGEL RAPHAEL

So many beautiful healing souls healing each other. Also, when you do healing work on your own soul, on your own self, it has a ripple effect of healing many others around you, whether or not you are aware. If you are at a place in your journey where you think perhaps your life is small because it is focused just on your own healing from past trauma or even past lifetimes, know that the effect of such healing is quite great on those around you. Even those you walk by in the grocery store, you might not be aware how much you are affecting others. You might not be aware how much you are affecting others by doing this work, this self-healing work.

Similar to, but not exactly like in physics, the vibration of different atoms although in different places in the planet can mirror each other instantly. Somewhat similar, others perceive on an energetic level the change in you. And then they understand how to go there quite instantly. For that just follow your own impulses towards greater light and understanding for yourself.

The doorway that you make will not be the only one for humankind. There are many of you on this planet now, some human some not, who are opening these doorways, and serve as the signpost or the neon sign that says: "Hello, there's an open doorway here!"

Some are physical portals, which would fit this metaphor, and some are not—they are just energetic states of being like those vibrating atoms in physics who can mirror each other. Once the energy has shifted in that way other beings instantly understand how to get there also.

# SITTING AT THE ROUND TABLE

## ANGEL RAPHAEL

This is Raphael, angel Raphael. Some of you have known me as archangel. So to avoid confusion, this is the same angel—there are not different, lesser and greater Raphaels in the angel territories. We do not have the hierarchies that you see in us. So "angel" works fine to let you know which type of being is speaking, but we don't consider ourselves to be in tiers or hierarchies; that as a human construct. Understandably so, because the human world was itself quite hierarchical until just now—just a few moments, days, years ago.

You are coming yourselves into a time of understanding that hierarchy is quite useless to you as an evolving type of being, as humans. We urge you to consider this as things begin to feel stale or outmoded in the way you relate to each other—look and see is it because there is some old hierarchy in place which doesn't make sense anymore. Because if you are no longer either being subjugated by someone else, or trying yourself to subjugate someone, the very notion of hierarchy doesn't make sense. Even from an efficiency standpoint, it doesn't make sense. If you were to say: "I am better at this task, so I'll do this and you're better at that task, so you do that,"

that's division of labors or inspirations. It's not hierarchy; it's something else.

To suppress people in this way, to create this enforced "lesser than" structure we suggest is not so becoming to the humans you're growing into. So you might want to look at that in your own worlds to see where there is old hierarchy that feels stale, or outmoded. Or where do I feel like I am being suppressed in a way that doesn't make sense anymore—where I was quite happy before to be slotted into some groove there, but now it feels uncomfortable, like I'm being squished into place. In those cases, you might want to look at restructuring within your own organization, or in some cases, leaving a place that is so devoted to staying the way it is and creating more circular structures. Structures where like your round table example, no one is really the leader. Whoever is speaking is the leader in that moment—the focus, the respect goes to them. But there is not someone who is leading all of the time.

As foreign as this concept might feel right now, within 10 years, or much less, the very idea of this kind of structured, hierarchical leadership will feel so foreign and removed. That will be the history lesson, not the round table. We are not saying that Arthur and his knights are coming back here into humanity, but that method of shared leadership—where each can be the hero in the moment when they are in action—is more pleasing to the growth of sentient species. There's no need to have some overlord experience.

We understand, the transition to stop leaning on those you had respected so much is a little bit painful, just like leaving behind the parents. It's not that you then put those that you had respected so much into a place of disrespect or into a box or shun them. We are not saying this. We are saying to recognize that it is your time now to come into leadership of yourself and to stand as equals with those respected beings. Let us say it that way, since you are so used to hierarchy. It's not quite how we would like to phrase it but that might help you come into a time of respecting your own inner knowing and at the same time not feeling you need to burn down the structures of those you had respected so much in the past.

It's not that you need to leave the people, the jobs, the structures that you're in, but a period of renegotiation is required. And here we don't mean a power struggle, but new daydreaming, new believing what it is that you want to be to each other.

## SOVEREIGNTY

### ANGEL RAPHAEL

Humanity is coming into her crown now. So many of you have begun to see this imagery of sovereignty in the form of a crown and are wondering what this means.

When as a race you are come out of subjugation and you are looking around to see: Who is the next master? Who do I believe or who do I follow? Because that is all that I have known. And all that my parents and grandparents had known.

The symbol of the crown is a message to you that you are to follow yourself. You are to be the sovereign. It is not that you are to be the subjugator of other beings. We sincerely and dearly hope that humanity does not tip over from freedom into wanting somehow to subjugate others. And we don't see this but we want to be clear when we are talking about crown we are not talking about sovereignty over anyone else.

We are talking about coming into rulership. We are talking about coming into being a full and sovereign being. And being full and truly who you are without any impetus—negative influence from the outside that is telling you to be anything other than what you dearly wish to be, anything other than what you hope and desire to be in this moment. It is fully, fully your choice, what and how you want to be as you live out the rest of this lifetime—for you personally and for humanity as a whole. So please do consider yourselves now sovereign beings, because you are.

Despite the fact that there are so many angels and other beings around in beneficial ways here to help you, you are guiding us now. That is why we tell you it is good to be clear about what you wish for. Because we are not going to tell you. We are not going to tell the sovereign being what to wish for, what to hope for, or what your purpose is here. So please look into yourself for these answers, for this sovereignty. And don't expect necessarily that you have the answer right away. It's new to you to consult yourself as ruler. So have compassion, but know that you have come fully into your sovereignty of being.

It is your time to play and be exactly what you are, what you wish to be, what you wish to come into. It is fully and truly your right to do this. It is fully and truly your time. Even if it will be a little clumsy here with the body making its changes and some days of fatigue, and some days of third dimension pulling heavily upon you so that the body can have some rest in its ascension. Even with that rocky time, you already are in your full sovereignty.

So don't wait. Please don't wait to make wishes, to restructure your life as you wish it to be. Your time of sovereignty is here already. You do not need to wait for any more signs, any more astrological events, any more battles to be won. You have arrived in your moment of grace and brilliance. As full humans, it is your time to rule over yourself. To have your free and sovereign choices. To have your free and sovereign will.

Much of what angels will be telling you in the coming years will be this message over and over in a variety of ways. You are free. It is your time to choose. It is your time to wear the crown. Not to have power over others, but to take your own power back. To live in a land full of people wearing crowns, and celebrating together.

~

COME into the sovereignty that you are, and seize this moment for what it is. You are now—in ways you were not before because of these unfair restrictions imposed upon you—you are now these sovereign creator beings. And you have come into this time of complete freedom over all of the aspects of your life.

What does this mean to claim your seat, to claim your power? It means ignoring for a moment all of the questions and doubts that your mind is going to raise about how hard things were in the past, how you tried this thing you dearly want 20 times and you're not going to try anymore, how it would take too long, you're too old to start now . . . anything that feels like a list of don'ts and reasons why you shouldn't begin. We ask you to ignore that voice. The mind has its place. It is a beautiful functioning organ. And it remembers these times of slavery, and it has learned that is the way the world works. Part of your role here as a sovereign soul, taking your seat at the table of sovereign beings, is to ignore a little bit all of these messages of the mind. It has done you a great service in helping you to function in this world. It does not need to be discounted entirely. But when you hear it start on those automatic lists of doubts and reasons why there's no way you could be as free as the angels say you are, it's time to put a pause on that voice of the mind and just experiment. Try for yourself. Try something new. Try allowing yourself the bravery to wish again, to hope again.

Many of you feel beaten down, in a sense, from having tried so hard over so many lifetimes and failing here on this Earth plane. But truly what you have come into now is such a different way of becoming. It is a different way of emanating what you want. So really focus on what it is in your soul that you want. Not what you think is impossible. Because you perceived accurately at those times 10 years ago, 30 years ago, what was not possible. It is not that you misperceived it then. It is that we don't want you to carry that memory forward and assume things are the same way, because they are not. And that is where those pain points arrive where that shell of our old life feels so uncomfortable for a little while. This is grace in a different form. If you were to feel quite comfortable with the old ways, you could spend the rest of your life—going back to the metaphor of a prison cell—you could spend the rest of your life quite comfortable in that prison cell, not realizing the door is open. We want for you to know the door is open, and to walk through, to truly experience yourself as a sovereign mastery being who can create anything, truly anything, in this lifetime moving forward. The old rules do not apply. They absolutely do not apply any longer.

And the heaviness that many of you are feeling now, that sort of overburdened feeling when going about your usual functions, is a clue. It is a key to knowing that you are truly not meant to go around staying in that prison cell, decorating, and trying to make it better. You're meant to step out into something new. What that means—something new—is very individual for you.

Another hallmark of slavery, perhaps you were given no choice, or perhaps you were given two or three choices. So you had the illusion of some free will. And now things are so unlimited, it is a little uncomfortable. Because no one is telling you what to choose, including your angels. We are not here to tell you what to make of your new life. We are just here to tell you that you are free to create anything, as long as you are not intentionally harming other living souls (plant, animal, human). As long as you are not stealing from others to make your new reality. For example, setting off an atomic bomb so that you can claim that country has your own. As long as you are not using a bulldozer to claim your space by running others over, then truly you are free. Anything that you can claim as your own power, as your own delight, as your own right to create in your life, is truly yours. Instead of taking from other humans, plants and animals to make this possible, why don't you work with them? They are also delighted to be in this time of new freedom and would like to play with you in this.

# PART VI
# THE END OF CONTRACTS AND DESTINY

# THE END OF A LIFETIME

## ANGEL RAPHAEL AND ANGEL ARIEL

*Angel Raphael:*

You are about to step out of the confines of this lifetime existence. You will still be in these body forms (unless you choose otherwise). In lifting out of third dimensional existence, you are shedding a lot of karmic ties that were holding you into certain patterns in this lifetime. It is very similar to when you die from one lifetime and then you have a full set of new choices. What should we create from here?

Although in the three-dimensional reality, in the karmic reality of what you are in in this moment, things have gone stale and died, ready to die, that is good. The timing is good, because that means that phase is completed, and you are ready to lift out into this whole new lifetime although you are still here in a body.

You might find, since there will be unlimited possibilities, that your choice would be very different some months (let's say less than a year from now) than it would be today, because you will not be the same beings, although you will be inhabiting the same skin. And that is not to say you will be a walk-in either. But that you will be freed from those karmic ties which are holding you into a certain life pattern right now.

What is happening for many of the planet right now, it is as if this lifetime is ended. Even though you will continue in the same physical body in the same lifetime. So the choices to restructure your life are that big, are that open, where you might decide to keep some things, maybe to keep some things as a hobby, if they still make your heart glad. But you are not required to keep on with the same goals that you had in that past lifetime. So very, very similarly, it is a time of reset. You have new choices here. Of course, some will choose to continue on the same path. And some who are not sensitive will not realize that this choice was open at all, and they might feel a sort of sudden dissatisfaction with the career that they always loved so much. So people will face this, will perceive it, in different ways.

Please be open to these dreams and wishes that spring up now—either as unresolved from childhood or as new interests—and entertain them, There's no rush to decide this week: what is your next life going to be? The timing will happen quite naturally and become more and more concrete as you move forward. So you might even test out different things. For example, if it was something about the environment to go to a class or a meeting, and see does it in practicality, we mean in physical reality, is it enjoyable when you get there? Or was it just an idea in the mind that sounded good. And if you go and you love this meeting or this class and you continue, then you meet friends in that, and you find a job in that. Then you see your life becomes more and more concrete around that new goal.

So it happens quite organically. It's not that the blank slate is only here for a week and you must choose and then your life becomes solid again around the new reality. You build it little by little through your own tests and trials—meaning, not that you are tested, but that you test out different ways of being, different ways of thinking, new job avenues perhaps, and see if you like it. It is compassionate in that sense. You are not being asked to choose and then there is no return.

It happens gradually as you move around in these new spaces and see if you like them. However, they do become more and more concrete, the more you reinforce that that is what you want. So 20 years from now, if you had changed to [a focus on] environment, for example, and you wanted to change then to horseback riding, yes, it is possible, but it might be a little less fluid than it is now.

We can say generally change later on in this lifetime, becomes a little bit more like change was let's say a year ago. Very possible, but it takes some concerted effort to make large changes like that in the life scope. But now, just now, it is quite easy to make those large changes. Now is the time to be wide open in your thinking and your allowing of yourself what you can have, what you can experience. Free choice will always be there, but fluidity of your world will not. [It] could be a little slower to create change in in the future or more dramatic.

It is also unnerving for most [people]. Because before you had the script, you had the rules. You had the ground rules, the game plan, so you knew what world you were operating in. And now it is so wide open that it is a little unnerving—except perhaps for a few who love chaos—because it is so unstructured at this moment. So the unstructured-ness is what makes it so fluid and free. And at the same time, we understand having lived such a structured life up till now why that is unnerving.

How do you find, in such a wide-open space, what you might want to be now? One thing you can do for yourself is to have a sort of ceremony sometime when you have a few hours on your own. A sort of the ceremony of looking backward at your life as if you were floating above your life and observing: what worked, what didn't work, what lessons did I learn, what lessons did I not complete, feel frustrated maybe that I never achieved or was able to face fully or complete? This could be done in meditation or writing meditation or speaking out loud, anything that feels comfortable. Sort of a eulogy, if you like, to the past-- the life so far. What are the big themes? What are the triumphs? What was achieved and could then be set aside, like a trophy on a shelf, and doesn't need any more attention? What is still maybe needling you that it never got satisfied as a life lesson or something learned? That's a good starting place. Look at what the themes are. What are the things that you want to carry with you into this next phase of life? Marriage, for example, or some job themes, some friends, some challenges that you feel like, I never got to speak up in this way, I'd like to still manifest some way for that to happen in this lifetime. Both the joys and the frustrations, those things that you feel are unfinished that you want to carry with you.

It could be a list, it could be a narrative to yourself, or simply a meditation. It doesn't need a specific structure. But to review the lifetime as if it was a stage that is now done. Lives are like that, in movies and also in real life, when death occurs, it is in the middle of the afternoon, or it's sometime in the middle of a project. It is not a neat ending where everything is finished. So the soul decides to take a few things with it, and to leave many, many things behind. The soul also decides to take some people along, of course, if the other soul is willing, into the next lifetime. It is very much like that. Just sifting through. What from all of this do I want to keep? And what things do I want to just observe: Oh, the arc of this story or this lesson was complete, I don't need that one anymore. Recognize, acknowledge that for yourself that some learning lessons were finished. So you don't need to keep carrying them around. Those identities that allow the learning lessons to happen, no need to keep all of those necessarily. And then some things, as we have spoken, that were jobs could become hobbies. So it does not need to be so black and white: I must keep this as a full life goal or discard it entirely. Some friends might move to occasional friends. And the reverse of course, some people you just met might become dear soul companions. Like that, just sifting through, what are some pieces you want to let go of. It does not need to be in a dramatic way. You're just making the decision first. And then you will see that the circumstances in your life present themselves quite nicely and easily to let go of a friendship, for example, or a certain place of employment. The universe is so ready to support those changes and movements in your soul landscape. Once you make a decision to move on from something or to amplify something in your life, you will see those occasions arise to make that quite easy for you. This is not meant to be a difficult juncture at all. So that is one piece: to look at from the current life, what do you want to bring with you?

Then how do we address how do we look at the wide open of what might be possible from a soul that is used to being so constrained and being given only limited options? One way for you to do this quite sweetly and easily--so instead of traveling around and visiting other workplace—is to watch movies about things that you admire right now. Things you are curious about. Step into that world for a half hour, a few hours. And see what that informs for you. It is sort of a conversation with your energy field and that possibility. What does it feel like? Does it lead you to more curiosity? Or is it off-putting? If it is off-putting is it just the characters in that movie or was it the whole setting, the type of job? Very playfully, just going to the movies or the theater or reading a book about something you're curious about, so that you can play fully interact as if you were in that world for a few hours and see if you like it. That is the easiest way to try out a whole range of opportunities in a few hours in a few weeks and months. Being very playful with yourself, because it is so unlimited you don't need to feel that the logical mind needs to make a list of what is possible based on your skill set based on your resume. . . . None of that applies in this broad brushstroke thinking. Of course, some of that will apply as your world becomes concrete around your new goals—people you have met before, job experience can be utilized to make that happen easily. But truly, it is not necessary. Those old rules of how things can be achieved, how jobs can be gotten don't apply anymore. So that will be easier than you think—those kinds of transitions—and easier than it was last year.

If you were to look at other people, whether you know them, or they are projections (for example, a celebrity or someone that you don't know but you have assumptions about) and you find that you are jealous of something, that could be a nice fun clue for you here. So you were taught for so many years to avoid jealousy and it being evil and so forth. But jealousy is a nice clue to say: "Ah, I wish I had that." Not that you wish to take it from that person. But I wish I had that myself. So as you look around in the grocery store even, in your classes, and you have these projections about people—and for this, it does not matter at all if they are accurate—but there is something in them that you wish you had: more purple clothing, or life by the sea or whatever it is. That is also a nice way to start building possibilities for your new landscape. What pulls you with this little jealous ear? Why can't I have that? But take it in a more innocent way. Because you can have it now. And you are not trying to take it away from a person, just use them as a sort of role model in this. What are the fantasy things that you wish you could have? Let it be quite playful and large or small, as you craft to this new reality.

We just want to reinforce, to be innocent with this. And by innocent we mean, children are not aware of the limitations on things. When you ask them what they want to be, and they say: "I want to be a firefighter" or a ballerina or the president, they are not thinking about all the obstacles that might be in the way there. The parents perhaps are, and have very fixed ideas about where to steer them. But we would like you to be that innocent, as if your perception of the world was: whatever takes my fancy is something that I can live in as reality. Because in fact, that is true. That is why we suggest this idea of movies to play in, because the adult mind doesn't go into fantasy as easily as children do. So it's a way of accessing those playful ways of thinking about, imagining yourself in very different worlds, different environments, different jobs.

But it does not need to be of course all career focused. As adults, we tend to think a life must be built around career. But that also is one of the things that is changing in this new reset. You might choose other things: love lessons, passions that you want to explore, to be a landscape painter, or whatever it is. You are not limited by the practicality of: How do I make a living from that? And it might be there are two separate tracks in what you create. One that is money and one that is passion. And it might be that in this new world you are creating, there are different rules. And not all artists are starving, to follow the painter analogy here. So at least in your first few weeks, months of thinking through this, please do come again and again to the innocence of a child. Really, if I could have anything... do I need three legs for this to happen? Let it be as outlandish as it needs to be in this daydreaming stage, because that is how you create something really new in your life, and not just recreate something similar to what you were imprisoned into in the past. Allow it to be very, very innocent and free. And the practical details come later. The dream part is more important.

The programmers of your world, to follow this analogy of a video game, to come back to this, the programmers in your new world being your angels and guides (to put it more simply, of course it is more complex than that) can worry about the whys and hows and the ins and outs of how to program that new reality into being. Your job as the creator of this new game you're in, is to design it—design the themes, the colors, the things you want to learn there, what it looks like, what the life experience is about. You don't need to know the HTML code behind the game or how long it will last or what is the cost to build it. What wiring do I need? None of that is your concern. You are the overarching creative director here and you can delegate those practical tasks to others.

∼

ANGEL ARIEL:

In that time in between lifetimes the sense of time, the sense of urgency is not there. There's this beautiful kind of dreamy exploration of: What would I want to do next? Which souls from my past lifetimes might I want to reconnect with? Or what type of new soul or experience might I want to bring in? There's this beautiful kind of sifting through, but it's not rushed. It's very, very similar right now. You have these souls who have been so dear to you in this lifetime, and you are introspecting: Well, do I want to keep that one around longer, or was that enough for this lifetime? Or, maybe I could keep them around, but we could switch up roles. There's no rush to decide this. But again, this feeling of disconnect could be expected. It's likely to feel uncomfortable, but it doesn't have to be viewed as a negative, more just an expected side effect. Truly, humanity has never been in this position before where you are still here in a body, but you have as much choice as you did in between lifetimes. It's a new kind of puzzle to navigate.

The good news is that because you are processing these attachments, or lack of attachments, now, when some year you come to the end of your life, it's going to be much easier to process out of this lifetime. Because you've already let go of generations before you, and decades of your own life. You're just pre-processing here.

# RENEGOTIATING & DAYDREAMING

### ANGEL RAPHAEL

You have come out of a structure of having been limited to maybe two or three different careers given your karmic skill set, and now you come to a time when it is truly unlimited—despite your age, despite where you are on the planet, in a country that admires freedom and enterprise or not. You have unprecedented freedom. So you do not need to be that career path, that identity, even that family member if you don't wish to anymore.

The options here then are within the structure that you're in. Let's say within family structure, for example, marriage and children. If your contracts had ended with these beings in a karmic sense—you learned what you meant to learn from each other, but most importantly, you all came into this time of freedom in the same moment—then it's more like you are people at a bus stop. You know each other very well, and you might decide to all get on the same bus together. You might decide the love is so strong there, you want to keep going on your journey together. But you're also quite free to move in different directions. And you're also quite free as a family to get on a different bus than you planned.

It's not that you need to leave the people, the jobs, the structures that you're in, but a period of renegotiation is required. And here we don't mean a power struggle, but new daydreaming, new believing what it is that you want to be to each other. It's important to realign with: What are your new wishes? And those can change of course over time. Just recognize you're not bound to stay with what you came in as a sort of contract to do with each other, what you had agreed on before coming into this lifetime. There were these freewill contracts that you entered into freely before coming into this lifetime. But then they became a little binding once you came here. So that's what we mean by contract with a marriage partner, for example.

Now you're still in the same house or the same bus stop as this person. You either feel distance or love for them. And you recognize the contract isn't there anymore. So it's really your choice as freewill beings: Do you want to keep going on the same road? Or do you want to stay together and go to a different road, or move apart into different freedoms. Understanding that this is from a sense of completion and dissolution of contracts, and not from a sense that they have failed you or you have failed them.

Many, many people are going to feel a little disoriented, let's say, lost within their current life. And if you don't recognize the disorientation comes because all of these structures have been dismantled, then perhaps you're looking to your job, your wife and thinking, it must be someone around me that's creating this feeling of why I feel so lost. It must be something wrong with the structures in my environment. Truly speaking, what is wrong is the lack of structure in your environment, that's what feels so unfamiliar and uncomfortable. Freedom right now feels quite uncomfortable for most of you, because you're not quite clear what is going on. It just feels so new.

# DISSOLVING CONTRACTS

## ANGEL RAPHAEL

*P*lease understand, as we have entered this beautiful new era on Earth, that contracts in a karmic sense are dissolving. When you have a situation like a marriage or a long-term business partnership that was set up according to what these two souls wanted before coming into this lifetime . . . now you come to this juncture in human history, where all of those bonds, whether positive, negative, or neutral, are dissolving. So what does this mean? It does not mean that all relationships dissolve. It means that you now both have much more freedom of choice to recreate what you want to be to each other.

Of course, one of the options is leaving. But when the contract—the reason for being together—is no longer there—the initial reason, the things you wanted to learn from each other, and so on—if that is all done, then you have this tremendous freedom to recreate your story here. It's almost like if you have seen those actor and actress pairings that you see in many different movies. Well, here you are those stars of the show, and if you'd like to stay together, fine, great. But you have the total freedom to change genres here. If it had been feeling like a drama, you can switch it up to romantic comedy, or however you like, more of a documentary, lighter feeling. There is tremendous freedom, even with the same people, same cast of characters, to create a new story here.

That can be done intentionally with both. And if that feels too threatening, for some reason, it can also be done one-sided. You can recreate your part of what is it that you want in relationship. What do you wish to grow and learn from? It is a beautiful moment, however, to do this together. There's more power, of course, if you are in alignment with what you wish. Understand that, although it's a little frightening in some ways as a couple to approach this because there was that security, that sameness in holding on to each other and not having to reevaluate that, there is beautiful freedom in new directions. You could move together without dissolving that bond.

Then when you look at work or friendships that same freedom is there. Even in something new. Let's say you decide to move in a new direction. You can still continually recreate. Things are also not so fixed as they once were. When you are creating a new circumstance, work or otherwise, friendship or just something coming into your life —a tangible thing like a car, for example—you can still shift those things once they are in motion, once they are played out. It is different than the kind of karmic structure that you're used to where once things are in motion, it becomes difficult to impossible to unravel or change the direction—where you had freedom, perhaps, to start new things, but not so much to change the old ways.

Here, it's different. It's more like a holodeck where you can change the rules at any time. That could feel unsettling if you're wanting to know what the rules are. Or if you look at it from the other vantage point: You are completely in control of your world and all the situations in it. There is great, great freedom in that to finally have the things you want. And perhaps to wish for new things that you didn't dare to desire before because it was too disappointing even to think about because they were so far outside the scope of what you could imagine for yourself.

Truly, there is tremendous, tremendous freedom in this time. Those around you might not yet be caught up to the fact that this is the case. This is the interesting thing about having human evolution at this moment. This type of freedom, as we have described, is accessible to everyone. But not everyone sees it yet. Most people are not yet taking advantage of these new freedoms. And even when you become aware of it, the trails of habit and fixed desires are so entrenched there, it takes a little while to get used to something new, to get used to freedom. It's only for that reason that mastery takes a little while here. It is not because there is a limit to what you can access right now. But there is a limit to how much you are willing to bend your own concepts of reality on any given day. And that makes sense.

There's no rush. There's no rush to come into mastery in this. It is just for you to know it is a new era truly on Earth. It is not hype. What you create now is truly up to you. And it was not in the past. Yes, there were these methods for manifestation or breaking free from certain situations. But they were very, very hard roads and not so accessible to many.

~

YOU HAVE the opportunity within marriage, and we are speaking collectively here, to rewrite your roles. It might be fun in a playful way. Not that you need to make this like a workshop or something where it's intense, and a lot of time is spent. But it might be fun, in a playful way, to daydream together: What might we want to be together since we're not fixed in what we had decided coming into this life? Since we've played that out, do we just want to continue that? Does that feel great? Or do we want to add a little of this, a little of that?

It's not that you need to plan out the whole rest of your life, in terms of your relationship together, but you might start to playfully imagine and daydream together. Gosh, if it's not this, what is it? What are we to each other? And what things that we haven't considered, both from our personal likes and dislikes that we just have put aside for so many years because we understood as a couple we don't do that together? Are there any of those things we want to revisit? Or just new things, new curiosities to explore. So in a playful way, you might start to write some new little pieces of script. Oh, wouldn't it be fun to do this together? We've never tried that. That kind of thing. Not planning for the next 20 years, but daydreaming and playing with: What else could we do together?

In this time of dissolved contracts, you can also rewrite those habits and roles about who always does the dishes and those kind of things. Take a moment to revisit that. Again, not to make it heavy, but to feel the freedom from patterns there. To try new things, and just have that lightness with each other as if you were newlyweds. There's no reason to make big changes. But it just might be fun to create new, not assume the same patterns must be followed.

# CHILDREN

## ANGEL RAPHAEL

Very, very similar to a marriage contract, you chose these children. Knowing each of you wanting to be at a certain age, let's say, and developmental place, coming into this widely changing Earth at different vantage points. You as an adult, perhaps chose to be an adult now so that you could experience the huge change—because it's quite dramatic and lovely, although yes, it sometimes feels like upheaval. But certainly something just incredible to behold, from an adult standpoint of recognizing the change and seeing how much beautiful change is here.

From a child standpoint—those babies coming in now—many, many of them are coming in with the knowledge that you will need, humanity will need, to survive and thrive and learn about the new dimensions you're coming into. Children are coming in now—this is very generally speaking, not all children, but many of them—are coming in now with the gifts, the sighted abilities, particularly, to see the other dimensions that you now have access to. So they become the ones, when they are old enough to articulate it, to help humanity understand what are these other dimensions really on a very practical level?

If you know some young children in your life now, you might think they're a little spaced out or not paying attention to you when you're speaking. It's probably because they are seeing fractal energy in different dimensions; there's quite a lot for them to pay attention to right now visually. And you are just one visual element, one voice among all that. So you don't need to worry if you're the parent of young children, that you need to find some special education right now for them to fit in with the world as you know it. They are here to show us all how to fit into the new world. So the children now are coming in with something quite else.

The age you are at this time of change typically makes a difference. Because it has something to do with the role you wanted to play in this time on Earth. If you had children, for example, who are 20 and 12 now—so more like adults, but still really your children, your babies—then this question of contracts becomes quite interesting, because you have over these years developed very fixed patterns with each other, some annoyances and some beautiful pathways of love and so forth. You also, similar to marriage partners, now have this ability to completely change any of those patterns or to keep them in place if you like how they are. It's not that your children then disappear from your life because the initial contract had been completed. There's much more freedom there, both for you as a parent and for the child, to experiment with. From the child's perspective, perhaps not being so locked into that identity that you've both come to see them as—are they the disruptive child or the quiet child, something like that. Now they have more freedom to play with. "I don't know. This quiet child thing isn't really working for me, I'd like to be rambunctious for a little while."

So for children, also, it's a time of exploration. And you might be surprised that your children start to behave in ways that are unfamiliar to you. Again, it is likely not because there is some intervention that is needed here from an education sense or behavioral sense. It is likely because on a soul level, these children are recognizing the freedom they're in and starting to experiment with, in a healthy way: "Well, what am I? If I'm not bound to be this personality that I knew myself to be, what are the other choices? Maybe I'll try that out." As a parent, the more that you can give freedom to that expression—it might come through fashion choices, or hobbies and friends—to really just let that be and not hold the child to: "but you've always loved ballet, you have to keep going." Whatever it is, allow for that great freedom in the children also.

For older relationships, let's say siblings of adults, you again have as much freedom as you would within a marriage contract. So your sister or your brother now that has always played this role, perhaps not speaking to you for 20 years, or being the needle in your side or being your best friend, but the one who was always better at everything than you were, whatever it is that maybe is ripe for some change there. You can also welcome in a change there because that contract, let's say that play or movie, came to an end. The credits are rolling there.

But similar to those actors and actresses who appear in multiple movies—you find them together again and again—you could still be in a movie or a play with your sister, your brother, your friend. But maybe you're going to change up the roles a little bit now. That's where the freedom is. Of course, you can also choose: "I really had enough of this person." But we want to be clear why we haven't really talked about the end of contracts that way, is that's not what it means. It doesn't mean you have to walk away from these people in order to find your new freedom, in order to find who you are, or to move into these other dimensions. No. But you're likely to feel a little detached from all of the situations in your life for a little while here, because it's like the anchor has been removed.

Now if you're a helium balloon, instead of something that's anchored with cement, it's very free floating. You can go anywhere you want, but you can float along with the same helium balloons that are your family now, or you can drift in a different direction. It's really up to you. But it will feel different. It will feel less anchored than it once was.

With children, of course, there are some differences because you came in with responsibilities as a parent. And if you have very young children, say you have a seven year old child, would it be all right from an angelic perspective to say: "Well, that contract is done. So I'm going to walk out of the door and leave that child behind?" No, we don't see that as a loving response to the end of contracts.

The same way that you would not walk by someone who was hurt on the road side or a baby who was dropped at your doorstep, whether they were yours or not. You do have some responsibilities as a human to care for the others in your sphere. Even if in the case of the baby dropped on the doorstep, it is to bring it to the next hospital or police person. You're not going to just walk by and say: "Oh, that's not mine. That's not my responsibility." And so if you have children now, you're not going to with the excuse of being "spiritual," walk away from all of these responsibilities and say: "Oh, well, that's not mine anymore. The contract's done." No. We trust you are mature enough to recognize that those beautiful beings in your life still need caring for.

For the most case, when you talk about children at the end of contracts, it means freedom from those fixed identities. I'm always the bossy mother, you're always the scolded child, or something like that. It means freedom from those patterns of the way you have of being with each other.

## GUILT & JOY

### ANGEL RAPHAEL

There is this human capacity for guilt when it comes to contractual relationships or commitments. Let's say you have put 20 years into a healing practice. Or you have a lifelong marriage partner, that was your understanding. It's been 30 years or one and a half years, or whatever it is, and suddenly, things energetically are so different. The first human response is typically this guilt, this sense: "I must remain bound, because I signed this contract." Whether you mean, as a soul, "I signed this contract to be with this person," or as a soul, "I put in this great commitment and years of schooling towards Reiki," whatever it is, and "now I must fulfill that commitment. I said I'm going to. There's people who need my help." You get where we're going here, right? This very heavy energy that feels like: "I must do this, because I made a commitment, and I need to follow through." There's a lot of "I" statements. And there's a lot of weighty feeling of guilt and feeling bound to a contract.

If you had come into these contracts in freedom, truly in freedom, then you are able to leave them in freedom. Let's speak a little more about this. All of you if you're old enough to speak and understand these words now, at the time when you were born into this lifetime was not a time of freedom on Earth, for humanity. So you learned viscerally, energetically that the way of being a human is to be in bondage—to be under contract, but in more of a slavery way, more of a way that didn't serve you.

To put some layers of misunderstanding here, and to have you play along with this game energetically, you were given this misunderstanding that it's quite virtuous to slave away your whole life giving away everything, receiving nothing, feeling depleted, and that is the most virtuous, saintly way of being. This is primarily what we would like you to shake out of.

If you were in freedom, and you wanted to help someone, it just happens that way. It happens out of love and delight. And then they're ready to move on. They don't need you to suffer the rest of your life in order for them to be uplifted by your gift—whether it is a healing gift or a gift of relationship. We are not saying here that we want all of humanity to move into what was called "free love." We don't mean be with someone for a little bit of pleasure and then move on. That's not what we're saying.

We're saying that this pull of this false kind of humility, saintliness, suffering lifestyle, was a trick. It was a ruse to keep humans happily struggling along in this sort of slavery time. So we're out of that now. It's not so important to detail all of the ways of how that time worked. But it's very, very important for you to know now that you are free from all that. Of course, if you wish to, you can hold on to it if you want, but we're suggesting it would be helpful to remove this whole layer of: "I need to suffer in order to be virtuous in this lifetime. I need to fulfill every single obligation that I committed to 20 years ago."

And we're not telling you not to keep your promises or to start lying to people, but to fully reevaluate now, in a time of freedom: "What in my life am I holding on to out of habit?" In this gloss of, this feeling of false virtue, that it's saintly of me to stay in this bad marriage, for example. It is saintly of me to continue with my Reiki practice, even though I don't get any joy from it anymore.

You have been misled into feeling that joy is a sign that you are somehow some frivolous pleasure seeker. Joy is such a pure, pure experience of divinity. And if you are having trouble choosing now. If you are feeling any doubt about what kinds of things are positive for you now in this time of freedom, follow joy please. If we can give one general piece of advice it is to follow joy. When you are faced with this choice of what looks like suffering and saintliness (as you have been taught what that means), and what looks like a joy, a joyful expression of reaching out to someone, giving to someone, lending a hand, laughing with a friend, whatever that might be . . . It still might be quite a gift of your time or your gifts or your energy. It still might be 20 years with the same person. But if it's given with joy and freedom, that we would say is serving you. If it's given out of a sense of regret, and guilt and false pain, all those things, it's time to recognize you don't have to stay with all of that. That was a trick. It was really, really a false understanding.

And there's this layer of vanity with it. "When I struggle so hard, when I give so much of myself, if my life is very hard, than I am very saintly and virtuous." So here's the vanity piece. The ego piece is: "I am so long suffering. I will be rewarded for this. I have come into a state of higher than others because I can endure this kind of suffering." That whole line of thinking is false. It was meant as an entrapment. And it worked very well. But It's time to come out of that, please. We do strongly suggest—it is always your free will to choose it or not—but we strongly, strongly suggest coming out of this false pretense of suffering.

That having been said, if you're in a marriage and you entered it lovingly, but it's feeling stale, or stuck right now, let's look first at the very playful way. Let's say your partner is also feeling the great energetic changes. And he or she is also looking at you like: "What is going on? Should we blame each other? Is it because of our relationship we feel this way? What do we do now?"

Here is our relationship advice, angelic relationship advice for this time. Can you come into a place of daydreaming together? "Okay, let's come at this from a place of completion. It's not because something went wrong, but because we completed what we meant to be to each other before we came into this life. We finished all that. But you know, I still love you. And you still love me. And we're still growing and evolving. So why don't we stay together? And what would that look like? Could we have a different pattern about who we are to each other? Could I have a little more freedom to do my work? Could you have a little more freedom from my interfering in your mental space?"

Whatever it is, if there are those pieces in your relationship that feel weighty—where overall you feel delighted about keeping the relationship but something feels stuck and old—daydream together. "What about . . .you remember you used to have that hobby, and then we stopped doing it because I never liked that? Could you show me that thing 'cause I feel like I want to try skydiving now." Whatever it is. Explore with great innocence. There might be some new things you want to do to with each other.

It's playful, it's playful. It's joyful. It's not so much the seriousness of: "Well we better write a new contract and be bound to it for 30 years." It's much more playful and joyful than that. It is more about understanding that you have this freedom to be something else, even within your existing relationships. Because the initial contract is complete, you have the freedom to be anything you wish to each other. It might be that you want to stay the same. That's absolutely within your free will to both choose that. But we do want you to be aware that you have the free will—the effortless free will—to move into other ways of being with each other.

# DROPPING ANCESTRAL LINEAGES

## ANGEL RAPHAEL

In a very deep sense, it is the end of the lineage for all time for humanity. This is something that can be perceived from two directions. Some perceive it as an Armageddon kind of end of the world. And we mean what you have already been through, we don't mean that there is some other big change coming. Some perceive it as the beginning of the Golden Age. So it really depends on how you perceive it. In part of this huge change for humanity, sea change for humanity, all of the lineages are being dropped. What we mean is, all of these karmas, you could call them, or DNA stuffed with trauma and belief systems from the past, you are shedding those when you move to fifth dimension. You cannot carry those lineages with you.

There is a heaviness there that is being dropped or left behind. Either if the soul stays in third dimension, when they leave this lifetime it does not carry over then with them as a soul to the next dimensions. Or for those who are still in body here—whether or not they are having children in the past or in the future in this lifetime—they have this choice, fundamental choice to walk out of, really step out of, not just their own personal contracts in this lifetime, but the whole lineage. The tremendous freedom of no longer needing to carry around the slavery and trauma of your ancestors is a good thing from our perspective. It's not something you really want to gift to future generations.

# WEALTH

## ANGEL RAPHAEL

Within these contracts, many of you also had contracts about wealth and money, what type of life you were going to live. Was it one of opulence? Was it one of squeezing wealth from others? Was it one of just getting by? Was it one of being a free vagabond not worried about money? So you had a kind of contract there, or script, character identity, around money as well. That has also dissolved.

Just because you had a pattern of "can't afford it," let's say, that doesn't mean that you have to walk around with the pieces of the disintegrating "can't afford it" contract and keep trying to read what it says there. You can just let it drop away. And then it really is your choice. Do you want to come into more opulence? Are you comfortable how you are now? Or would you like to downgrade even to more simple living, if you feel trapped by all of the formality of opulence that you've grown up in? Wealth in that sense is quite neutral. So it's up to you. Do you wish to carry on with the same levels of wealth that you've had so far? Because you're free from that structure also.

Even if there are wishes for a life partner, or a certain type of wealth, or a certain identity circumstance that you have wished for continually for 20 years or many times and stopped wishing because it hurts so much. Understand that you're in a very, very different playing field now. And we encourage you to have the heart strength to wish again, for the exact same thing that you have come to believe you can't have. Wish again, at least once more. Understand you can have it now. Really your world is unlimited.

# WORK

## ANGEL ARIEL

With work, as with personal relationships and with the third-dimensional reality, the contract that was binding you to that situation is done. The time of all of those contracts of this lifetime are done. But that doesn't mean you can't stay in any of those circumstances. You have the freedom to pick and choose. "I like this part of this." Or, "I'll just stay here for a while coasting along until I figure out what to do next." You could expect that same feeling of emptiness or just not quite engaged feeling. That doesn't mean something's wrong. But it does mean that likely you will find something else that has more joy to it. In the meantime, there's no harm in continuing in any of the existing circumstances.

There's no rush to jump off into something new. But, you will find it. There will be those days or moments and hours when this joy of inspiration and new ideas and new opportunities comes flooding towards you. So it's all right to wait until it feels clear about what to do next. In other words, if you don't leave it right now, it doesn't mean you're stuck with it for the rest of the lifetime. It just means . . . like when you take the moorings, the anchor off the boat, it's ready to sail at anytime but it doesn't have to. It's just not connected to the dock anymore.

## SOULMATES

### ANGEL RAPHAEL

*L*et's look at this question of soulmates. There is this belief in fate. That there is one person I'm meant to meet, or maybe three in a row, or however many you like to feel are your soulmates in this lifetime. There is this fear. The old fear way of thinking about it is: of all the millions of people in the world, what if I walk down the wrong corner on that day, and I miss that person? There's this fear-based way of thinking about soulmates that believes there's something that can be missed, something that can be lost easily. That it's much more easy to lose or not find than it is to greet that person.

But if you were to look at the significant people in your life, whether they are romantic partners or not, looking back now wasn't it quite obvious that that person was going to be in your life? The energy of meeting that person, wasn't it so bold in your life? Of course, family members are a little different because you didn't feel that meeting if you don't remember your birth so much. What we want to say is for those who have decided before coming into this lifetime to meet, to interact with certain souls, whether it is one soulmate or many, those arrangements are quite strong. You don't have to worry about accidentally walking down the wrong street and missing that being. That's one piece of this concept of soulmates.

Also understand that with this sea change in humanity, all contracts are dissolving. So it is your choice. You can still keep them, you could still keep your meeting arrangement, still show up at the right time and place to meet that person. But you might also recognize, consciously or subconsciously: "You know, what I was drawing into my life isn't a very good fit anymore. I've grown a little in a different direction. And I really wish that I could meet this type of person."

So yes, truly the free will is there to change still, even if the contracts were there. That was not the case two years, 10 years ago. We are just using this as a rough time frame to say, the reason why this is hard to conceptualize is because you did grow up in a different world. And now it's changed. So even those people who are in romantic partnerships now, you have this beautiful freedom to look at each other and say, could we be something new to each other? Because we've both grown and I think we can make something even more beautiful here. Instead of being in the place that we had agreed on before being born we were going to be together. There is a lot of freedom.

And yes, it is that beautiful paradox that you can absolutely create everything down to the specificity of hair and eye color. And there are other freewill beings here. So you're not creating out of a holodeck in a sense that person who walks down the lane is real, is a real person that you have drawn towards you. That is a science it might take some years to dance with until you fully understand: How is it that I am master of my world, and there are all these other masters of their world interacting with me, these freewill beings?

In some sense, it is very complex. But in another sense, it's very simple. If I as a being decide I really love the color purple, I now want to go to this room over here, because it's purple. And I really enjoy that. And I wish I could be around other people who like purple. Well guess what, other people are gravitating toward that room because they like purple too.

So it's also very simple. It can seem in the mind like it's not possible. "How do you change because I have this contract and" . . . that's the mind getting into so much confusion. All of the possibility of complexity is there, but it can also be quite simple. And that is your choice—again, this world that you're creating. For some it's much more entertaining if it's very complex, and there are puzzles to figure out. So you might be creating that kind of world for yourself. For some, they just want simple. So you can have it any way you like.

# PART VII
# ENLIGHTENMENT

# WHAT IS ASCENSION?

## ANGEL RAPHAEL

*The blind men and the elephant:*

When we speak of ascension it is ascending out of ego which is this shell, this container, identity container you are in. And so if you are one shell on a necklace, then instead you perceive all of the strands and all of the variety of stones, and the clasp on the necklace all at once.

Instead of defining which piece of the puzzle, which piece of the universe are you, you are perceiving wider and wider: What is the universe? Like the blind men and the elephant.

*From Adria:*

There is an old teaching fable about three blind men trying to figure out what an elephant is when encountering one for the first time. This tradition appears in Buddhist, Jain, Hindu and Sufi texts, and I will recount it briefly in my own words here.

One man is standing near the tail. "I know what an elephant is," he declares. "An elephant is like a broom." The second man is standing near one of the elephant's legs. "No," he says. "An elephant is like a tree." "You're both wrong," says the third blind man, standing near the elephant's trunk. "An elephant is like a snake."

We can have such certainty about what we are perceiving, based on our viewpoint. But are we seeing the whole picture?

∽

ANGEL RAPHAEL:

Like the blind men and the elephant, the more you can perceive all the different sides of a thing—the smells, the sights, the tastes, the intuitions, the knowingness, the touch—the more you can perceive all of this about a creature, a situation, the more you are in resonance with what we would call ascension, which in another frame of reference means perceiving things quite clearly.

# YOU ARE THE TAPESTRY, NOT A THREAD

## ANGEL RAPHAEL

The ego takes hold of this concept of enlightenment and says: Ah, "I" understand it. "I" need to escape. "I" need to escape from the illusion of this world into something called enlightenment, which is full "real" understanding.

The ego carves out this false idea that the individual soul is going to escape from some kind of mass disillusionment. This is close to the truth. But the ego—in the way that it does, out of performing its function as defining itself as an individual soul—sees things a little askew.

You are in a world where that is one thread in the tapestry. And the sooner you realize that you are all of the tapestry, not one thread trying to escape, you see conceptually those two take you in a different direction. What would the thread be trying to escape from in the tapestry? It is the all-that-is. It is the whole picture, and all perceptive layers of it—the silk, the picture that the eyes of the human can see perceiving it, the weaver, the energies of the weaver going into the tapestry, the colors of the dye, the character of the pigments from earth that created that dye, the volcanic eruptions and earth formations that created the minerals that created that dye.

You are all these and many more layers when you look at this tapestry. So what is it that you would escape from? It does not make sense. You are not here an individual thread wriggling out, trying to wriggle out of imprisonment of tapestry. You are instead wriggling your perception outward from perceiving only the boundaries around you.

Instead of perceiving the boundaries around you, where your thread touches other threads, where your pigment differs from other pigments, which part of the picture of humanity are you painting? Are you part of some goddess's hair? Are you part of the calf's foot? Are you part of a pathway? A piece of dirt in the picture? These kind of perceptions of defining the individual strand in relation to surrounding strands in the overall tapestry—that takes you in the direction of definition, which is ego. But when you perceive yourself as one of many threads—and just perceive it, not judge it, just perceive yourself as one of many threads—and you perceive the colors, the different colors, and you perceive the different scents, the different time frames, state of mind of the weaver . . .

These are analogous, these are not literal, but come very close to the literal energy fields you are playing in and beginning to understand. So yes, you are a thread, and <u>yes</u> you are the tapestry.

The way into ascension in this phase of enlightenment is to become what you already are, which is the tapestry. Not to attempt to be something else. What if you pull the thread out of a tapestry? Let's go very directly to the metaphor. And the thread is lying somewhere on the ground. It is still part of the tapestry. There is no way for it to be other. There is no possible way for it to be free from what it is. If you burn that thread, it becomes a burned tapestry. Or a tapestry that is now partially in vibratory form in smoke. But it is still what it always has been which is part of the all. And the all is always changing. That tapestry is going to age, is going to be eaten by moths, is going to be destroyed in fire or flood and dissolve back into earth and mineral, air, into intention, into energetic impetus, into creativity, into boastmanship of those that want a beautiful tapestry on the wall. So it dissolves back into what it always was—all of these different strands and energies together. Then what are all those strands and energies once they are released from the tapestry?

Are they free?

Or are they exactly what they always were—the fields of interplaying energies telling a story together at some moments in time or space, defined a certain way. Always changing on a molecular, on an energetic level. Always changing. No matter how static the tree or the tapestry looks for 100 years, it is never the same one moment to the next moment. So your job as a piece of this, thread of this tapestry, is to perceive not just your own strand. Is it aging? Does it smell with mold? Has it faded in sunlight? Is it still hanging on tight to the threads around it or is it loosening? (So not becoming free but just loosening.)

Perceive not just how the individual thread is relating to its environment. Perceive the whole picture throughout all of time. And then you are in enlightenment. It is a perceiving of all that is. It is not "I am." "I am" always has a qualifier. I am the thread. I am part of a tapestry. I am weaving or interwoven. I'm being transformed. I am enlightened.

This is why you will never hear this phrase from an enlightened one. "I am enlightened" does not make any sense. It is the only qualifier that does not fit behind "I am." "I am" is ego. "I am" is defining itself through these various pathways of perception, but only where the individual body let's say touches up again sunlight, texture, time of day, season, age. How is it perceiving itself in relation to its own boundary, its outer shell? That is "I am" that is ego.

The "am," the perception of all layers of being simultaneously is what we would call enlightened. You still perceive yourself as an individual thread. You can see where you are in the picture. But you can equally see where some other threads are in the picture, and the aging of time and the energies and the dyes that we spoke of. So you become one piece of the elephant you are perceiving, and not the whole thing. And when you become a piece of the elephant and not the whole thing, you are in complete harmony with the changing nature of the unchanging one.

Let us call it a void—the unchanging one.

It is the opposite and the exact same as the tapestry, which is the void expressed, which is the void perceived. So, you have these options as you look toward enlightenment. Two main pathways, let us say. There are many teachers. There are many methods. There are many disciplines. But there are two main pathways (let us call them for now) —ways in to correct perception. One is through the void, letting all of these perceptions and attachments and beings, claims to being, dissolve—this void. And the other is to embrace every single thread, every single way of perception.

Saturation of perception in a way is a very still place, but it is a perception of chaos and ever-changing molecules. So, it is infinitely entertaining. The void is also a way into what you would call enlightenment and we would call being in the all-that-is.

Where are angels on the spectrum of enlightenment? We are still perceiving ourselves as beings of light with functions to perform, individual functions to perform. But at the same time, we do not see judgment, see ourselves as higher functioning than ants or other beings. We perceive ourselves in a category of things and we perceive many different viewpoints at once.

Is this enlightenment? It is, except that we can only communicate from our category (viewpoint). That in a sense is ego. We can only communicate from angelic viewpoint. Angelic viewpoint happens to be very close to the all-that-is because it is so non-judgmental and because its perception is so broad. Not for any reason of hierarchy, but because the very function of angel comes closest in the human realm to this perceiving widely.

*From Adria:*

I need to take a quick segue into a personal story here, so that how the angels speak about this experience below can be put into some context for you. Recently I became much more aware of, and sensitive to, the needs of the insects in my home. It didn't make sense to me that some ants shouldn't eat the drop of honey on the outside of the honey jar that I wasn't going to eat anyway, for example. They went away again when they were done. They weren't visible in my kitchen at other times or otherwise bothering me. And was there really a problem with a spider (non-poisonous) living behind my bedroom door? Then I started to wonder if I was being too much of a pushover. Was I supposed to assert my authority to live in my home? I couldn't see why I had more of a right to live there if we were peacefully co-existing. Just because I pay rent?

I had been puzzling over this for a while and then when Raphael was giving me this message about enlightenment this moment in my life was used as an illustration, and in the angels' playful and practical way, Raphael asked for the spider example to be included in the book.

*Angel Raphael:*

The more you can perceive this dissolving in . . . or we would say allow yourself to be distinct, but perceive everything else at the same time . . . That is what you were beginning to judge as being a pushover —not wanting to disturb the spider behind your bedroom door. Being very cautious of it. Is that being a pushover to everyone else's will? Should you be asserting your will to have a spider-free home or to have a blank wall behind the door without a web on it? Why would your individual assertion of will be more important than any other ant-sized assertion of will? That is what you're beginning to perceive.

And that is not, in fact, becoming a pushover to others. It is a widening of perception. So, it is from our perspective quite good to begin to perceive others' wishes as equal to your own.

Then how do you—out of free will—ever choose your wishes? It does become more difficult. It becomes more difficult to decide what you might want when there are so many ways of perceiving.

It becomes quite delightful to understand the nuances here of egoic structure and how it influences the path to enlightenment. How it perceives it quite incorrectly. Wanting to remain King instead of a thread—a changing thread in a changing tapestry.

# THE VOID

## ANGEL RAPHAEL

The other main enlightenment pathway is through the void, or into the void you might say. It is not that there are only two pathways to enlightenment, but most of the methods, techniques, and ways of getting there could be categorized into one of these two: the perceiving the all-that-is, or the void. They are contradictory and paradoxical approaches that lead to the same "place" of being.

Is this really what I am? That is the essential question that begins to take you towards the void. Am I really defined by the identities I see here? Mother, friend, whatever type of profession is often top of the list . . . is that what I am, really? Am I this body? These two legs, these two arms, these eyes, this hair, whatever fashion it is styled in? Is that what I am, really? This house, this car, the type of clothing that I wear —these outward expressions of my personality or my wealth—is that what I am, really?

So, if you come to the conclusion by asking any of these questions: "It doesn't make sense that that's what I am, really, at the core, at the heart of my being." Then what are you?

If the body can be changed; if the lifetime can be changed (and here we are speaking about reincarnation and also the daily and yearly changes to the physical self—aging, illness and so on); if there can be that much change and fluctuation in those most fixed things about yourself—the body, the identities; if you can take on a whole new career; if you can become mother-less, or become a mother, when you were not before; if all of these somewhat fixed identities and identifications with yourself can be changed, houses can be lost and gained and so on, then: What am I, really?

You must ask yourself, if you want this way in towards enlightenment, this is the pathway. Continuing to ask this question: What am I if I am not this changeable thing? If I am not—let us put it very frivolously—if I am not this hairstyle, what am I? Because you know the hairstyle can be changed as much as can so many, many things about you, even in these days the color of your eyes, the color of your skin, the shape of you can be changed.

So, what am I, then?

And you come to this beautiful, wordless place in asking that question in so many different ways. The answer there is a sweet silence that is full of everything and nothing but in this way in its characteristics is more of an absence of definition of self.

If you want to take a broad view, scientists would speak about the space between atoms, between people, between worlds, as the defining characteristic of matter itself—the space between things.

Is that what you are? Are you space? Are you air? Are you ether? Or are you something even less than that?

In the potentiality of all things, when you come into the heart of creation, creation is always birthed out of this nothingness. It is quite extraordinary. If you cut a seed in half there's nothing on the inside. So how is it that you are born out of nothing, out of the air or something less than air? That is the great mystery of the void.

∼

THE ALTERNATIVE to perceiving the all-that-is, is to move in the opposite, so called opposite direction, toward the void. This is also a pathway into enlightenment—understanding or enlightenment experience, both.

If you are in the all-that-is, another way of expressing that is that none of this is real. Meaning, none of what can be defined and perceived from an egoic standpoint, from an individual standpoint, is real. Necessarily that must be false. If you are not truly a separate distinct individual, then what you perceive from the viewpoint of separate distinct individual must be false in some way, in some measure, if not totally false.

Some traditions take you down the pathway of saying: "not this, not this." God is not this. God is not this. God is not that. Anything you can perceive, that is not God. That is how this tradition proceeds with taking you down this pathway toward void—the beautiful creative potential, let us say, of the all-that-is or God depending on how you want to define it.

It is a little bit like this chicken and the egg. One does not exist without the other. The all-that-is does not exist without the creative potential. But then again, neither does creative potential stay very long without creating something. Both of these are like the two wells at the far ends of the infinity sign, they coexist and they respond to one another. It is not that one of these—void or all-that-is—is true and the other is incorrect. They are both separate and opposite ways of perceiving the same thing.

So, if you are to approach the void as a way into enlightenment, if this feels more natural, more becoming for you, then as you are walking through your day or perhaps in more formal meditative times, you are aware that things are dissolving, or that they are being misperceived because they are not real. You are bringing your awareness again and again towards nothing, towards void or empty or potentiality.

It is not a lifeless void, it is a void sparking with creativity and life potential. But within itself, it carries nothing. It is the end point and the beginning point of life depending on how you view it. It is the force that allows the human soul to continue living after the body has disintegrated or disconnected from the soul. This ability to live without matter is what the void contains. That is its mystery and magic if you like.

The void is also the all-that-is but it is unexpressed in that moment, when it is void it is the potential for all. It is the power to create all. But it is not manifest all. That is the only difference there. When you are perceiving from the all-that-is it is also ever changing and unlimited, but you are perceiving its manifest self in that moment.

If you are going to close your eyes and disconnect from the relative world—the world that you can perceive through your sensory experience—and come into that sometimes soft and gentle, sometimes very fiercely defined void, you are willing then to let go of all identities, all concepts of yourself, all outer forms, in order to reach the potential, untapped potential of creation itself. Either way that you approach this—you see as we have expressed it as the wells, the pools, within the infinity sign—either way you approach this, you are still within the same system of reality or God or divinity, however you like to phrase it.

It is not that one path takes you opposite from the other. They are apparent opposites, but they are contained within this infinite being. A being that is expressed and a being that is potential for expression.

If you are residing for some hours or days, or weeks in the void, it is those moments when in meditation, you lose track of time. You lose track of self. You lose perception for some time and only realize that has occurred when you come back to it and perceive again: "Oh, I am sitting here. I must have gone somewhere or become nothing for a little while. I didn't realize. I had stopped becoming aware that I was sitting here meditating."

That is the experience, the gift, of the void. Of course, sometimes when you lose awareness you might be traveling inter-galactically, inter-dimensionally or something else might be going on. But in most cases, let us say, you are cocooning in the void there for a little while, taking rest and respite from the sensory outward experience. And because all of this is God, unexpressed and expressed, it is no less "spiritual" to approach divinity through the senses, through the outer world, and is no less "worldly" to approach divinity through the unexpressed void.

# DIMENSIONAL SHIFTS VERSUS ENLIGHTENMENT

◈

## ANGEL ARIEL

The step from third to fifth dimension is different than steps along the enlightenment journey. If as a soul you've chosen: for right now there are some things I'm learning in third dimension that are going to help me in my enlightenment journey, and I need those right now or I want those. That doesn't hold you back from ascending into the higher dimensions in the future. But it also doesn't hold you back on your enlightenment journey. They're slightly different things.

It becomes a little easier once you're in the fifth or other lighter dimensions to zoom forward a little faster in the enlightenment journey. But they're not the same thing. Someone who makes it to fifth dimension might get very wrapped up, for example, in instant manifestation, and just spend the whole rest of their life on that. There are a lot of toys and bells and whistles, let's say, potential distractions in fifth dimension. Where it is, by and large, a lighter, more exuberant experience, it is not by itself enlightenment. So those are separate journeys.

## ENLIGHTENMENT PATHWAYS

✥

### ANGEL RAPHAEL

We would like to speak about enlightenment from within. Many of you are used to following systems or pathways of what we would call enlightenment from "without," from outside yourself—a prescribed path that says you must do this thing, and then that thing. And it's the same for everyone, and it's quite linear. And this is the way it's always been done.

If you were living in a very structured time, as humanity was from some years ago back through all of the generations of your ancestors, that makes sense. It's almost like if you were living on a jungle gym kind of a bar structure, and someone had made a map: if you crawl out this way, that's the easiest way out. So within those kind of structures, it makes sense to have a set pathway out. But when the structures are torn down, and you come back to that empty lot that used to be jungle gyms, and you have this map that says: This is how I climb out. Well, you could spend the rest of your life in frustration just looking for the first step in the journey because the bars are no longer there. So not only are the old ways becoming outmoded, they also become unnecessarily frustrating because the structures that were in place that they were responding to or reacting out of are no longer there. So those pathways are not just slower, or outmoded, they no longer work because they're built upon structures that no longer exist.

One of the byproducts of losing structure, of coming into freedom, is that enlightenment pathways now are quite organic, and they come from within yourself. So what does this mean? Does that mean literally inside your body? No, it does not. But it means that as a soul, given the pathways you have followed, given the pathways that are in your DNA structures, given the life circumstance you have set for yourself, there are certain obvious energetic pathways up and out from your situation. So it is a little different than rising from third to fifth dimension; all of you reading this are already on that journey. Not everyone on this planet will choose to lift out into fifth. But certainly, if you're curious enough read these words, you have made that decision, even if you didn't have those words for it.

There is a certain very visceral, very physical shift in dimensional reality that is happening within your generation here. Within these few years, you are physically shifting into fifth dimension and higher, and the abilities to travel more easily between the dimensions. But this is a physical thing; it's not necessarily an enlightenment thing. It makes it a little easier to travel towards enlightenment, because as you are dropping so many old structures and embracing freedom, there's a part of your soul that says: "Oh, it's that easy? Well, I want to embrace all the freedom!" Yes, we would say go for it! There's no need to hold yourself back to what we or anyone else is saying about what is possible and what the timelines are.

The basic movement that humanity is taking now doesn't mean that you are limited to only shift into fifth dimension, for example. You can certainly go higher, and those dimensions have always been available. But they are more readily so now. It is easier to lift up and out of where you are, because of these new freedoms. So let's consider freedom as the new environment you're in—it's very, very new for humanity to feel this.

While we are in freedom, how does enlightenment work? It is following those nudges of interior guidance. Sometimes it might come from words that someone else says that resonate so deeply that you want to follow that pathway, that energetic pathway. But most of the time, it's going to come from some inner knowing. And again, we are not talking about inside the physical body, but on a soul level, what is distinct to you, versus what you are being told or witnessing through the senses. One way of thinking about this "inner" then is things that are not perceived in a sensory way. But there are certain things that you know, and shifts that you feel that you can't explain based on what your eyes see and your ears hear and a sense of touch, for example. So that is a good shorthand to say, okay, that's what Raphael is talking about here, about inner light, or inner pathways of guidance.

We encourage you to be free to follow your own knowing. When a child grows up to a certain point, it is first a little fearful to step out on its own to walk to school for the first time on its own, or to tie its own shoes. There's that sense, first, of wanting to cling on to the pant leg of the parent: "Please don't let go." But very, very quickly, the child becomes absorbed in other things: friends at school, the ability to define their own fashion sense, or whatever it is. We're just using simple examples here.

You're in this moment energetically, emotionally speaking, that's a little bit like that—where you are being told, perhaps prompted from within: "It's okay, go ahead. Go out on your own." But there's a little bit of fear there. "Well, I don't know if I can, and I've never tried it before, and this is different than anything I've ever known." So be gentle, be compassionate with yourself. But at the same time, we tell you, you are free. You are grown. You are in this moment where it's time to start following your own advice, your own knowing about things.

So even if it doesn't match what you read in the newspaper, or what your husband is telling you, or what a book on your bedside table says, it's time to start following your own knowing. Even those teachers, which are so dear to you, which have taken you through leaps and bounds in this lifetime, may start to sound to you a little tinny, like they are speaking inside a structure of old ways and what they're saying no longer vibrates to you with newness, with aliveness.

We understand just like leaving behind the parents, that's a little bit painful, that transition to stop leaning on those you had respected so much. And it's not that you then put those that you had respected so much into a place of disrespect or into a box or shun them. We are not saying this. We are saying to recognize that it is your time now to come into leadership of yourself and to stand as equals with those respected beings.

Let us say it that way, since you are so used to hierarchy. It's not quite how we would like to phrase it, but that might help you come into a time of respecting your own inner knowing and at the same time not feeling you need to burn down the structures of those you had respected so much in the past. But perhaps it is time to walk away from them for a little while, just like our example of the child going off to school. Maybe it's okay to take a short walk on your own and just test it out. What does it feel like not to be within the structures of that old way of thinking? Does it feel better? Does it feel wrong? Just to test it out for yourself, really not to take anyone's word for it, including angels speaking here. We are suggesting you start to trust your inner knowing and trust those inklings, those energetic pathways that are opening up in you, that are beckoning you towards enlightenment.

Enlightenment, then, is a little bit like a magnetic pathway, instead of an escape route that you need to follow the instructions about. This more interior way of finding enlightenment that we are describing now feels a little bit more like a magnetic pull. It is not literally that. It's not that the highest status of humanity is to be magnetized or stuck to something else. But there is this pull. There is this glimmer of light, this sense of wonder and attraction towards enlightenment.

This is one of your natural states of being. In the beautiful love that creation became, it is always wanting to come back to itself. This impulse of creation.

You see this even in the three-dimensional world. Look at a wave in the ocean, how it strikes out so beautifully and independently. And then there is this pull, this undeniable pull back towards the source from which it came. Like that the enlightened pathway is this strong, magnetic almost pull. So you don't have to figure it out with the mind. The waves and those drops of water within the wave are not sitting there wondering: "Which direction should I go?" They just feel that pull. And it is strong, and very, very natural within you like that.

## RECEIVE YOUR ENLIGHTENMENT

### ANGEL RAPHAEL

Receiving is not limited to material possessions, or even states of mind or being. We want you to know that it is within your sovereign right and abilities right now to receive enlightenment. In a way, these small manifestations, these wishes and receiving, are a playground towards your enlightenment. For those of you who only want material possessions, you can stop there; it is your free will. For those of you who want to go higher in your energetic spheres, and help others to push forward gently into light, that is also available.

We start with practical examples. We speak about houses and cars and so forth, because that is attractive to many people. Today, we want to skip right over to the next step of what you might call manifestation and we like to call receiving. It is also time when you can receive your enlightenment, your full enlightenment. All it requires in this time, again, is wishing—being clear about what you wish to receive here in the energies. Are you ready? Are you willing to leave behind your old ways of being? Are you ready? Are you willing to come into your full enlightenment? Are you ready?

Are you willing to help others on their journey? It does not need to be both. Some people are only interested in their personal enlightenment. You choose. You are a free will being—that is our shorthand way of saying you have choice over the energies in your environment and how you wish to create moving forward in your life. It does not have to be about service to others. We just see this general trend for those who wishing enlightenment for themselves, they often wish also for service to others.

Even if your goals are more lofty like this, try out wishing for material things so that you can come into this shorthand with yourself of energy, of really playing with wishing for and receiving what you want, in playful ways. Almost like the world was a catalog and all you have to do is point to what you want. It is that simple. So learn that, practice that, and then point to the page that says full enlightenment and you can have enough belief within yourself to instantly receive it.

The time of work and struggle, so many uphill battles towards receiving what you want and so many times rolling backward down the hill and feeling discouraged that you have to start again, is largely done. We are in a little bit of a mixed energy field here. So some days you will feel that access to your enlightenment and some days you will feel stumped, like the old walls are in place. That is largely out of compassion for humankind as we shift into these higher realms of energy.

What you find is that the human system doesn't like to jump from where it was to such a high level overnight, which is why many people have been talking about waves of receiving new energetic ways of being. Some people call them codes. Some people call them shifts in consciousness. All of these from our perspective are the same thing, which is stepping into your enlightenment gradually.

So right now there will be some days where it feels like the shift can happen instantly, and some days where it feels like there's a block in place, and it feels almost worse than the old way out of contrast, because you're used to that instant reality, that instant way of stepping into your new being. So, have patience with this. It is NOT—we cannot overemphasize this—it is not a linear pathway. So, do not be discouraged if today you feel you are on the brink of this enlightenment and tomorrow you feel back to square one, or like you are in the emotions of your teenage self.

It is because, particularly now in this next year or so on the planet the energies are quite chaotic from your perspective, from your perception. (Take that advisedly understanding that angels are not in time so we do not do time predictions very well). That is designed out of compassion for the human system. It is not that you are suddenly in this random meteor field of energies and you need to fight or flight to find your way through to the gentler passageways. No. It is all designed like this to be chaotic and a bit disruptive because the human system does not like jumping so fast from one to the other.

That is why when you have these historical examples like the Buddha, you see someone meditating, building that capacity over many years. We tell you that it no longer takes years to build this capacity towards enlightenment. But the human system still perhaps does not want to make this instant shift. That is why the interplay of energies are as they are right now, where you feel so ethereal and light one day and then maybe two hours [later] or the next day you feel like a stone. So take heart. It is not you. It is not something you are doing or undoing. You have not fallen off from your meditation practice or otherwise unlearned what you know so well already. It is that you are in this beautiful chaos of energy so that your human system—this vessel you are wearing—can grow used to these higher energies. You have full access to them now, if you were to jump into them today now. Some of you are ready. And for some of you, it would burn out, fry your wiring system a little, metaphorically speaking. (We do not think you have actual wires. You are not a machine.)

Also trust in this: that your angels and guides and your own human organic self knows what it is ready for. So you don't have to mistrust, if you wish for enlightenment, that you'll get it too soon, too quickly, and it will burn you up like the moth and the flame. No. Trust that the time involved in the delivery system here of your wishes has everything to do with what your human energetic system can accommodate. So some wishes when they take more time (as you perceive it, time) have to do with this. It's a compassion to yourself.

So when you make wishes, whether it is for the car, the house or enlightenment, take the time factor out please. Please do not wish: "I want this house within 30 days." Or, "I want enlightenment now, in one hour." Instead, just wish for what you want. I want a house—like this, in this neighborhood, this large. And don't worry about: Is it going to come through money? Is going to come through a gift? How fast is it going to come towards you? Just be clear about what you want. And of course, in some circumstances, when you are being kicked out of another place or something like this, there will be a time frame. So you can add that: and let it be ready before you need to move out of your old location, something like that. There can be qualifiers. But we would urge you not to add time into your wishing. In fact, things can happen more quickly when you don't add time, generally speaking, because the human mind based on the experience of the lifetime so far wants to say that things are going to take at least a week, a month or a year. So you might be shortchanging yourself by adding time in when things could happen much more quickly.

We want you to know the full access of the energy spectrum is available to you here. Then you can trust that your angels, your guides, your own knowingness will bring you towards what you wish at the exact moment when it is most beneficial for you. So it is safe for wishing. This is a question that we often receive. "How do I know what to wish for or what is in my highest good?"

Be innocent like children in this. Not a bratty child, not a tantrum child. But remember the innocence of how children just know what they want so clearly. Be like that. Know what you want, because you do know what's in your heart. And trust that if something is not of your highest good, you'll get some message about why something else might be a little better, you can adjust your wishing as you go. This is not a one time wish. It is not a limited 30-day supply of wishing for the rest of your lifetime. Now you are in these new energies. Things will be a little less chaotic after this year or so. But you will still be in these energies of instant reality where you can create what you wish and receive it.

Feel safety in wishing for what you want. Don't worry so much: "Is this is selfish wish? Is it really for my highest good?" Follow the delights of your heart. Because in receiving small things like this, you learn. You build up that trust and that you really can receive the large things that you wish such as enlightenment, such as saving others from types of bondage, of illusion, and so forth.

# PART VIII
# WHAT ARE ANGELS?

# THE PRIMARY FUNCTIONS OF ANGELS

## ANGEL RAPHAEL

Angels have three primary purposes and some other abilities also. The primary functions are messenger—this is what we are most known for, for bringing messages of comfort or joy or a warning, whatever it is from that which you perceive as God or divinity. (We would say from the central soul or the core of being. It is not a separate distinct individual, the way we perceive of this.)

God is certainly not human shaped, but God is also not a distinct soul. God is our center—all of our center point in being. We have the opportunity if we like to move closer to God in our different lifetimes or to play in the field of God which is all experiences. For purposes of learning, for example, humans are not always aware of their connection to this center point, God.

Angels in that sense are quite close to God. Now again, we do not mean hierarchically so. We are not higher or better than humans. But we are more aware of the godlike nature that is central to all of us. We are more aware of the play, if you like, of energies—the all-that-is that is the field of God. So we do not feel so distraught or distracted by this feeling of separateness from God, because although we are not residing in the center point—what you might call enlightenment—we're close enough to perceive it and to perceive our role in the wider universes.

Angels are not limited to assisting humans. On this plane of existence that's what you know, because you are looking now from the vantage point of human eyes, and you perceive that angels are here to help you. From your perception right now, that's who angels are for. They are for humans. Angels do occasionally play the role of helping each other in those similar primary ways. Angels are available to other galactic systems. But right now we're a little more concentrated on humanity. Angels are not limited to humankind, but you will find them most often near humans.

Back to the primary functions of angel. After being a messenger, angels also bring healing or "divine" intervention. Being closer to this center point, God, angels can also see the manipulation of light, let's call it—how it can be used to create and destroy. So here is where you get manifestations of miraculous healing, apparitions of light for teaching purposes, and so on. Most often the manipulation of light because angels are in light bodies.

The third function of angel has to do with returning to the source point. For those who are attracted to the energy of angel, some of that attraction comes because of that proximity to understanding who and what we all truly are. When you are approaching this enlightenment pathway, often you find angels come to assist because they are more familiar with the ground between where you are and where you are going, let's say it that way. Angels can be a good guidepost or beacon towards enlightenment.

Those are the three primary functions of angel: messenger, manipulator of light, and beacon toward enlightenment. Some people use angels only for the second; praying often for miracles. Some in trying to understand the world they are in or get some guidance or belief within the structure of their life call on that messaging function of angels for some comfort, for some understanding and relief from the apparent illusion or opaqueness of the planet you are in. Those are some of the reasons and ways to consult with angels.

# NOT ABOVE

## ANGEL RAPHAEL

From angelic perspective, there is not a hierarchy of light. Many humans have come to this concept that there is human, and then above that angel, and above that God. And within angels all of these hierarchies. We do not, in fact, call ourselves "archangel" or those other types of titles.

As angels, we see ourselves as more light; we do not have the physical density of a human being. So there are distinctions, but we do not place ourselves above humans.

In the same way, we do not place God above because in our experience, God is a light that permeates all things, including angels, including humans, including chairs. If God is in all things, then yes, you are God. That is how we see it and we know that other beings see things differently. And we welcome those different viewpoints also.

## YOUR ANGELS

### ANGEL RAPHAEL AND ANGEL ARIEL

*Angel Raphael:*
Each human has angels who are with them—and we would say generally more than one—for their whole lifetime. These are angels who have been assigned to your care.

And then there are some moments in life when you have a gateway that is open. Or if there is a death in your family or something where there is either a great possibility for learning and joy, or great burden of grief, or transition, or confusion—then other angels do sometimes come in to guide and assist in those moments. So there are some angels that are with you for one day or two years, just for some little period of time. Maybe while you are with child, for example. There are those temporary assignments.

Then there are those like Raphael, like Ariel, whose names you know. They have been called archangels in many times, even though we don't subscribe to that title. The name of an angel carries great weight, great energy. You can call on those angels you know by name also. Each of these angels has different specialities—healing or heart opening, and so forth. So you can also call upon particular angels if you feel like you want that extra help.

Angels do love to give help, so please don't feel shy about asking. At the same time, if you don't know the names of your angels, they're already with you. You don't have to call them by name. You can just communicate with them either through thought or through words, through the feelings in your heart, and they will listen and hear you.

∼

*Angel Ariel:*

Although we use the word assigned, it was you who chose these particular angels before coming into this lifetime. And then they also chose that assignment. So there's a synergy, symbiosis of what gifts they have to offer and what you wanted to grow and celebrate this lifetime.

# ANGELS ARE LEARNING

## ANGEL RAPHAEL

Angels, like humans, have different modes of being. Angels for a long time were mostly employed in service towards humanity's higher good as battle angels, let's say. But angels are also guides, which is more what we are being utilized for now in this time of lots of question marks. And angels also have an innate nature of playfulness. So when angels are in battle, we are not going to see that playfulness as much. But right now angels are having the celebration of their lifetimes ! (Angels also do have life spans.) And they are in quite a time of celebration and joy.

Angels do not have the physical density of human beings. They are more made out of light, if you want to talk in physical atomic terms, but they do have a physical presence. And they are learning beings. Although you know of them as teacher and friend and guide, angels are also learning and evolving.

This is a great victory for angel-kind also—this time in humanity—because it wasn't ever certain that freedom was going to take place. Angels have also been battling, working towards this, guiding from within, so in different modes—the same as humanity has been working towards this freedom. Angels are also more either in their guide mode—mode of giving advice and clarity—or in playfulness just now because for angels, it is a time of unprecedented joy.

We understand humanity has not quite come towards being able to see with as much clarity what has happened. Many of you are still looking for the signs or the coming events, the coming freedom, when it has already arrived for you. So that is the irony here. But there is a little bit of growing into your new freedom, and then perhaps the celebration will also be there from the standpoint of humanity.

# HUMANS AND ANGELS

## ANGEL RAPHAEL

Angels were created, let's say, at the same time as humans more or less, in the Divine experiment of: "What could a human be?" Angels were created to help and assist. "What if," is the question, "humanity had access to more guidance and help than other creatures in the past?"—and that was the creation of angel. Angels evolved then to serve animals and others. But you will not find such a thing called "angel" specific to other intergalactic systems, for example. There are certainly many, many other types of guides and spirits and knowledge carriers and so on. But the human experiment and the angel one are very linked, which is why we had said recently angels are also growing. We do not need to have the physical adaptations that humans need for moving into the fifth dimension. But our role necessarily evolves as humanity evolves and becomes more free.

We are less of a guide and more of a library, if you like. We can help, but we are not pointing the way because we are not way showers. Humanity, some of humanity, has that function. We are an access point in, if you like, to divinity for those who seek it, and an access point to knowledge, or ideals, ideas about the world. But we are not pointing the way any longer. That was our role for a little while when humanity was seeking so much help and was in such a lost place as to need that much light to show the way. Now when all paths are open, our role becomes quite different. And we are learning this alongside you. We are also learning what our new roles could be and what freedoms that might offer to angels also.

# ANIMALS AND ANGELS

## ANGEL RAPHAEL

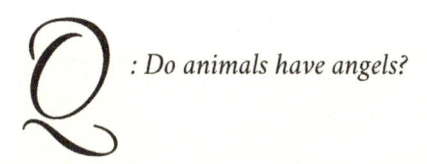

*Q: Do animals have angels?*

ANIMALS HAVE ANGELS, yes. Some animals have many angels because some animals have come in to serve on quite a grand scale. And they need a little assistance in communicating with humans and others, and angels help with that. One of the core functions of angel is communication.

Some animals have only one angel. And it is not that there is such a thing as a human angel and an animal angel. "Angel" is like saying light, a beam of sunlight; it is not really different when it is serving an animal or a human. Different angels are assigned to different animals and people for different periods of time. So they play a very, very similar role of guidance and protection, and communication generally. For animals, the angel of an animal often also has the role of helping the animal to communicate with the humans in its life.

# ANGELS AND REINCARNATION

## ANGEL RAPHAEL

Q: *Do angels have souls that reincarnate the same as humans or other beings?*

THE TIME FRAME is a little uncertain from your perspective because angels are not in time so it's easier to see a human take birth again and again when you are looking in a linear way. It becomes a little more confusing if you were to zoom out outside of time. You might think that was many different souls, not one soul born in different bodies. For angels you have to view from a very wide lens to see this, but yes we do reincarnate and sometimes leave [the] angelic realm. And yet there are angelic souls who wish to change a little something about themselves so they shed the current identity and come back again as angel and some stay on for some 200-400 years and then decide to move on to another galactic being lifetime and so on. It becomes addictive helping others but sometimes we do tire of this role and want something for ourselves. We get jealous, in a sense, of your ability to live life experience and then crave that for ourselves sometimes.

## CALL UPON YOUR ANGELS

◈

### ANGEL RAPHAEL

There is a lot of miscommunication about what angels are. Let us say in general terms that we are unlimited energies and communication devices [laughing]. We are ways of communicating love and messages and comfort, certainly. It is a way of translating divinity, which has no substance, into the substantive world. So, an angel is a way of edging yourself towards the experience of your own divinity in all aspects of your life.

That is why angels do not mind when you ask them about small questions, because each small word, each small moment in your life has meaning when it is focused on taking you towards your highest expression. And your highest expression does not need to look like anyone else's highest expression.

Many people have guilt or feel shy about calling on angels because they think angels are only there for times of cancer, great illness or crisis. This is not the case. Angels are unlimited, which means they do not feel burdened by little questions by millions of people at the same moment around the globe. So please feel encouraged to call upon your own angels, or those angels that you would like to name and call upon, for anything—for guidance in your day, for planting a flower, for being more in tune with your own divinity in that moment.

Angels are here to serve in that function of translating divinity into purposeful existence or practical reality, both. It does not have to look like your life's work or the greatest, most peaceful prayer to be something you call in an angel to help with. As long as you are not calling in angels to harm another, an angel is always happy to be there to play with you in the delights of this world.

You have heard the story, most likely, of the genie in the bottle. In most stories, you have three wishes from the genie. Of course for angels the wishes are unlimited, but the principle works the same. You must ask the genie for the wish in order to receive it, yes? Angels are quite similar. Although they can be there to protect and guide and nudge you in the right direction, they also must be asked directly if you want their assistance with something quite specific. In general, they are there to guide and protect you. But the more specific you can be in your requests of angels, the more specific they can be in their response. So instead of saying, "I really like cake" . . .(We don't think angels are bringing you cake. This is the best metaphor that came to mind.) If instead of saying "I really like cake," you said: "Please bring me a piece of chocolate cake," your waiter will have a much better time pleasing you. Your angels love to bring you what you want, what you desire, and also what will uplift you, of course. The more specific you can be in your wishes, in your questions to angels, the more they can give you specifically what you want.

～

*Q: Do we have to speak out loud to angels (because there's so much in our minds)?*

It does not need to be voiced out loud. But you are correct that the angels do not follow every thought in your mind or we would have quite a chaotic universe, even more so than it is already. If you have the capacity to be clear enough in your thinking that it is a wish or request to your angels, that is fine. It does not need to be voiced. It can also be written down. Clear thought is the same as a voiced thought.

Or a question can be meditated upon, sort of offered to the angels. It can be specific like the chocolate cake example, but it can also be an open question. "This situation is in my life and I wish to bring light or more joy or more peace to it but I feel stuck." And you can sit in a meditative way with that question and ask the angels for guidance or help. You do not always need to know what the answer is that you are asking for.

So it is not always specific. If you knew how to solve every problem in your life, then you would not be asking for help. In that sense, please do not feel that you need to solve the question before you ask for help. It can be an open-ended meditation as well.

# SEEING ANGELS

## ANGEL RAPHAEL AND ANGEL ARIEL

*Angel Raphael:*
Angels are physical beings, but not corporeal beings in the sense they don't have the same kinds of bodies as humans. They might appear sometimes that way within a human mind, as a sort of holographic projection from within that human mind, because that's what humans expect to see. So if an angel wants to communicate with you, and you're a very visual person, they might show you an angel cloud in the sky, or they might show you what looks like a physical human with wings, standing in front of you. Sometimes we appear that way, although we are not a cloud and we're not a hologram that looks like a human. But sometimes we show ourselves that way just to be clear, to give that message of grace, of hope, of love—whatever the guidance is in that moment.

For some people who are more auditory then we speak through words, through messages like that. For some who are more cerebral we might speak through words, where you open a book, what feels like randomly, and there's this message there for you that's so specific. Or for those of you who are more visceral, more related to touch in the way that you go through life, it's this feeling—this pull or gut feeling towards something or away from something. Angels have many, many ways of communicating. That's why if you're going to try to compare with other people's experiences, you might feel like one is wrong or right, or feel confused about what an angel really looks like.

As a being of light, we have that great capacity to dance and meld into whatever is going to be comfortable and easy for the humans we're working with to understand. It's not always visual. And sometimes it's more than one. Many of you have had this experience of thinking something, thinking about angels particularly or thinking about something quite joyful, and then in that moment seeing angel numbers on the clock. So it's quite playful.

~

ANGEL ARIEL:

Many of us are trained to think that the eyes are number one; what we see with our eyes must be true. Maybe number two is words or hearing. The knowing sense is usually quite discounted because it has no proof. It is a little more rare, but also true that some perceive information through their guides and their highest through this sense.

For all of you when you want to come into touch with your own guides and angels, and you all do have angels, and you don't want to be dependent on always going to someone else to ask: "What does my angels say?" Because they're your angels. They're there for you and with you all the time. So how do you tune in more?

One way is to learn what your language is. When you're speaking with other people do you really like to see them face to face? Or phone is fine because it's really their voice you want to hear? Or do you really like seeing things written down? When you just notice how you are with human-to-human communication, it'll probably be clear to you what's your favorite way of communicating. Start looking that way for communication from your guides and angels. If, for example, you really like things in writing—in in emails or books—then try using some books at home. Ask a question, open [the book], and see how fine-tuned you can get that way of communicating with your angels and guides. It's not that you should conform to someone else's way of communicating. Your angels are there in any case, whether it's as a gut feeling, or some other instinctive way. The time you thought was such a bother to be delayed five minutes and then [you did] not get into that traffic accident. Your angels have ways of making the important things happen or not happen in service of what you want.

Finer-tuned than that, when you are really wanting to communicate and delight in the communication with your guides, they are there for all of you. It is just coming into tune with: "How do I best hear them or see them or feel them or know them?" It will not be the same for every person.

We'll take this to a larger point in the playing field of humanity. Because free will is such an important lesson we're learning here, humans have decided to look different, speak different, have different tastes and desires in order to have this perfect playing field to play that out. If we all wanted hamburgers every day for lunch, it would be hard to tell if you were exercising your free will to eat that thing because that's all anyone would serve in any case. Who cares whether you are blonde or brunette? But there are these distinctions because then the play playing field is much more nuanced.

Along those lines, you have different ways of communicating with your guides and angels; it's just part of that variety of this free will playing field.

# ANGEL NUMBERS

## ANGEL RAPHAEL

Numbers have an energy. There have been those among you who are quite attuned who have given specific meanings to different numbers—a different meeting for 333, for example, than 444. Some of those are correct; sometimes you might find nice resonance in what that specific message is supposed to be. But on a pure level, on a visceral level, the angel numbers—which would be this repetition of three or four numbers that are the same like 1111 or 444—have an energetic resonance.

It's a little tricky to speak of this because some people use the word "codes," and that makes it sound like you're a computer program. Even we have used the word holodeck, but it is not that. You are quite an organic system. And yet, numbers do have this very magical outcome, chemical effect. When you see a number, it's not so much the meaning attached to that number, although that can be helpful and comforting, give some security to the mind. It's actually the vibration of that number and what it does to your physical system.

It's not important to intellectually understand: "Oh, what's the message then?" The message is the energy. The message is that energy of clarity, of love, of joy, of peace. Those are some hallmarks you could associate with angels, when they are not in a battle mode (as we are not these days). On the simplest and most profound [level] of what the numbers mean, it is a vibratory message gift to you from the angelic realms. So it is real; it is a real energy. And sometimes you might take comfort in looking at the difference from one number to another. But understand, that's filtered through a human understanding, which may or may not be clear. If it [someone's explanation of the meaning of different angel numbers] doesn't resonate with you, you don't have to worry; just take in the energy of the number itself.

The mind doesn't have to understand an angel gift, an angel blessing, an angel sighting in order for it to very deeply assist you in whatever way it was meant to. Many times, a part but not all of the message is just for you to know that angels are there for you. To not feel so alone, and to feel surrounded in the love that you are. Because you have many guides, certainly, in this lifetime. Not all of them are angel, but some of them are. You have many seen and unseen helpers in this life. The numbers are just one way that this communication is transpiring.

When you perceive a number on the clock (or wherever it is), to take an extra moment just to drink it in is quite nice. That's the way you can amplify what the angels, and sometimes other guides, are sending towards you. Think of them like little fairy godmother blessings. Just receive them. You don't have to understand them; just open your hands, metaphorically speaking. But of course, it's more with the eyes. Just gaze a little longer at those numbers and take it in. They are blessings in that sense. Little bites of alchemy for your system.

There are quite a lot of physical changes going on to enter a new world. Without a spacesuit, without a different kind of physical vessel, your physical body needs to undergo tremendous, tremendous changes in the next few years. And part of the ways this happens is through these numeric what some have called codes and we would say the vibrations that they carry. They are little blessings to help you align to what you're coming into, to help you grow into a stronger, more resilient physical vessel. Or more appropriate, let us say, for the time you are in.

# PART IX
# WHAT'S NEXT?

# GREAT CHANGE ON CELLULAR AND DIMENSIONAL LEVELS

## ANGEL RAPHAEL

*G*race, Grace and more grace is upon you. 2020 is a year of great change. The change happens on the cellular atomic level and in the energetic playing field, both.

Externally you can expect your world to align more and more with fifth and higher dimensions, and all of the hallmarks of those higher ascended levels, such as your thoughts becoming your world more instantaneously, less focus on the denser world, and more focus on lightening of your soul space, so to speak. The hallmarks of third-dimensional living which are falling away increasingly in the coming year are: struggle, linear thinking, and attachment to money.

These are not the only, of course, hallmarks of the third-dimensional reality, but they are the ones you might notice most in the coming year. When your thoughts become instantly your reality, and you can wish into being like that what you want, money becomes less and less important. So we encourage you to practice that—wishing and receiving—so you don't feel so fear-bound to the monetary systems and that old slavery way of being where you were deluded into thinking if you only worked hard enough for enough years you could get what you want. We would like you to have what you want now.

The fifth and higher dimensional realities make that possible. That is the wider energetic landscape you are coming into.

You have received that and perceived that already in 2019, but it becomes gradually, not suddenly, stronger. The gradual nature of the ascension process has to do with physical readiness, not with soul readiness or the emotional landscapes. On a soul level, you are ready already or you would not be reading these words.

This is what we meant when we spoke of atomic cellular changes in the physical being: the physical vessel requires quite a bit of fine-tuning to harmonize into the fifth-dimensional or higher dimensional realities. Your physical vessel in this lifetime so far for most of you has lived out its time in the third dimension. It is acclimated and designed for that dimensional reality. It is quite unprecedented that what is happening now is <u>all</u> of humanity is welcome now into this transition to the fifth dimension. Not all humans will willingly choose to go there. So they will be allowed, of course, to stay in third dimension. For those who decide to move upward the physical vessel takes some calibration (of course, a dimension is not up, but that is the conventional way of speaking about it).

This is the "bad" news, but only in the near term. What we mean is, this transition is likely to be felt. The more you can accept it for what it is and not believe you are all collectively having health problems at the same moment, the more you can be in a state of grace and acceptance for this tremendous transition. The physical body is likely to want to put on weight for this transition, again in the near term. This does not mean you will carry this extra weight for the rest of your lifetime, but perhaps for much of the coming year. The physical body is likely to have wild fluctuations in when it wants to rest and how much and when it is wakeful at what might seem to you to be inconvenient times (in the middle of the night and so forth).

When you are restructuring your whole physical embodiment to live in a different dimension, you need to understand, to be realistic about the fact that it is a tremendous, tremendous transition. Please be respectful of your body as it goes through this process and don't start hating on yourself because you feel you have become sluggish or fat. That is not what is going on dears. You are changing into something quite else.

On a soul level, on a mental level even, you remain unchanged. But the body on an atomic level has to go through as much of a change as if you were to go from breathing air to breathing water. Of course that is a metaphor; you are not going to be in an underwater Earth. That's not what we mean. What we mean is that your body is quite capable of this tremendous transition. Yet, you will feel it. It is a transition. It is a transformation of what you have known in your life 'till now to something quite new, reformed. Reformed in the truest sense. We do not mean lifted out of some kind of degradation or sin, but remade, reshaped, reformed in the most literal sense.

On an energetic level, you do not need to direct this process. There's very, very little you need to do from a mental or energetic standpoint to guide the body. This process is underway already for those of you who have chosen to move into higher dimensions. It is an organic one, literally an organic process. The same way that you trust that a baby in the womb or a flower coming out from the seed knows how to grow into something completely different than what it was two months or two weeks ago, your body knows how to come into this new transformation. This transformation has been ongoing already. For those of you who are leaders in this—meaning way showers, way finders, light workers who were eager and ready to be among the first to take these transitions—you might have been feeling this already quite strongly in 2019. For the general populace, they begin to come into these physical transformations a bit later than you did, beginning in 2020.

Why do we say then that it is a year of much grace when we have just described many symptoms that seem like they might feel unwelcome? There is tremendous grace in the potential of upliftment of the entire human race, or all of the human race that chooses this, to lift into fifth and higher dimensions. This is not something that has been offered or available before for humanity as a whole. Some individuals have made this journey or have come into this lifetime as a multi-dimensional or higher dimensional cloaked being. This is quite different. This is quite new. What you have been longing for, collectively longing for, in terms of upliftment of the human race is here. That is cause for tremendous, tremendous celebration.

# CHANGE YOUR WORLD

## ANGEL GABRIEL

Now is the time for you to create in your heart-space exactly what you want. Exactly what kind of world you want to be inhabiting. Exactly what kind of relationship spaces you want to enter into (or not at all, that is also your choosing). Do you wish to hibernate, in a sense, away from others, or do you wish to be with many, or just a few? How do you want to design your life?

You grew up with this false assumption that your life was designed for you. Or, you grew up with the belief that you could shape your own life and have reached many, many frustrating moments as your desires were thwarted. Now is the time to shape your own existence purely from your own imagination, purely from your own understanding of what is possible, purely from your own desire—heartfelt desires—of what should be, of what is.

Instantaneously you come into your New Earth, your new dwelling places, your new friendships, your new abundances. It is truly your doing how you will live your life from now forward. You have no one to blame but yourself if you are dissatisfied with the result. Change your life please if you are unhappy with how things are. Change your world. Not your worldview. Change your world.

Recognize that the world around you is responding to your mental picture of what you ask it to be. Do you expect frustration and anger when you go to work each day? Then you will find it there. Do you expect disappointment and a lackluster life at home? Then you will find it there. Do you expect miraculous change, healing, growth, newness? Then you will find it now.

It is up to your mind, your heart, your wishes to decide. It is no longer the dictates of any fate, any external being or beings, any creature—manmade or other—any programming, any false beliefs, any shortcomings. It is truly within your own understanding that your world around you is shaped and born on a moment by moment basis.

As you become adept at understanding this, as you become adept at perceiving this, you become masterful in shaping your own reality. You have that willpower. You have that power already. But you misunderstand and keep creating the habitual landscapes because your belief system tells you that is what is possible.

It is time to break free now from old belief systems, from old hampering of yourself. Do not hold yourself back from proclaiming what it is that you want. Do not hold yourself back from receiving what it is that you wish for. It is time now for you to create the world as you want it to be, and not respond to the world as you believe it has been crafted by someone or something else.

You are the creator being of your own world. You are the creator being of your own circumstances. You are the creator being of your own heart's wishes. It is time to take back the steering wheel of your own life.

# THE VALUE OF TIME

## ANGEL RAPHAEL

Not all worlds or all dimensions are in time, but yours at this moment—the third dimensional spaces and others spaces—are in time, so you experience your world this way. Why was time "created" in that sense? What is the purpose of being in time? We'd like to speak about this a little bit today, because as you move into fifth dimension or the accelerating energies on the planet Earth, if you have asked to move forward in one of these ways you're moving out of time.

From the collective experience, what does it mean to come out of time? And what was the purpose of being in time for that rather long experiment there in third dimension? Some of you have begun to experience already that when you have been practicing wishing and receiving or just daydreaming about how your life might be, things come to you in a way that doesn't make sense. If you were to use the vantage point of time, it was too fast. It happened too easily, too quickly. When you have days or moments like that, you know that is a very fifth-dimensional experience. So you're already dipping in and out of fifth dimension and other dimensional spaces, which is why some days it feels very disorienting, or very different from the third-dimensional reality you're used to.

It's not necessarily going to look visually different when you're in fifth dimension. It might appear you're still in your house, or your car, or whatever it is. But one of the clues that you are dabbling in fifth at that moment is that time doesn't seem to play a role. So you get things much, much faster than you would have anticipated if you were doing it the third-dimensional way—the hard way, or the way of struggle and time.

If it's so much easier, simpler, more joyful, in a sense, to be out of time —to be in a fifth dimension or other dimensional realm where time is not between you and what you want—what is the purpose of doing it the slow way or the time-bound way? There was a quote to attributed to Einstein (whether accurately or not) about time, in which he says something like: the purpose of time is so that you don't have to experience everything at once. This from our vantage point is truth, is the truth of time.

If you were to experience even this one lifetime, your growing up, your present and your future all at once—to really viscerally experience that—it's too much to process from a learning perspective. It feels too dense, too much there to manage. Whereas, of course, if you spread those tasks out over what we call time . . . Some seasons in your life, certainly, particularly with work, you felt too busy. But it doesn't feel like your brain's going to collapse back into a black hole because too much is going on in one moment and you can't process it all at once. So time has a value there.

We would say the purpose, particularly when you're looking at learning—and angelic perspective is often focused on learning, so you'll often hear us speak of this—if you are focused on learning, then it's easier if you can pull things apart—kind of look at them piece by piece. And time is very helpful for that.

One drawback, if you like to say it that way, of being in fifth or other dimensions that are not bound in time is you don't have as much simmering time, or reflection moments, to learn from what is happening. As you move into fifth dimension, perhaps you are feeling frustrated: "Some days, it's so easy, and I just daydream about what I want, and then it's there at my door. And it's so gentle and flowing and easy. And then some days, I'm just crashed back down into third dimension. That's what it feels like emotionally. And things are so dense and slow."

In those days when you feel a little stuck in third dimension or lower dimensions, you might just reflect on the learning pieces. That's one way you can use the positive qualities of third dimension. As you move forward on your path here, you will have more and more of what we would call fifth dimension, although some of you are also experimenting in higher planes of existence right now. (So again, you're not limited to only fifth. But collectively, humanity will move mostly into fifth dimension out of third where you mostly are now. So that's sort of a general truth.)

One of the ways you can manage this frustration you might have over the fact that you're not there already all of the time is to savor the learning in those moments where it's so slow in third dimension, and maybe you're getting a little bit out of the habit of doing and struggling all the time, so you're not so interested in going back into that mode. You can also use third dimension to reflect on the learning. Does that mean in fifth and higher dimensions that are not in time, we don't learn and grow? It does not. But it's more rapid fire. So for those of you who are comfortable with a slower pace, third dimensional learning is a little more obvious. Sometimes too obvious, you might say, for those of you who feel stuck in emotional moments from time to time.

We think some of you are feeling frustrated right now about time, how it seems to not at all be a barrier on some days or some moments and then it feels so weighty by contrast, when you come back down into third-dimensional living for a little while. One of the benefits, if you are someone who likes to think about positive aspects of whatever is in front of you right now, one of the benefits of having a little more time-space in third dimension is to have this learning reflection.

∼

*Q: Do the angels have any message for me as I navigate a very challenging health and financial situation?*

We've spoken in the past about the clarity of what you want. Then today, we're speaking about time. If you are clear what you want in this—financially and health-wise—that's one important component. And you don't need to feel that you need to waver in that. But if some pieces of that are not coming immediately eminently true for you, you could recognize: "Well, I'm in third dimension right now. I must be because things feel stuck, feel uncertain. I feel afraid. What can I learn from this? Because very quickly, more quickly than I realize I'm going to be out of this situation."

Reflect back on a time last year, or five months ago, where it felt completely impossible you were ever going to get out of that situation. Then somehow you did. Life moves on. Life has a way of moving forward, we would say. You are not going to be stuck in the situation you're in forever, certainly. And not very long. Almost like—from the perspective we're trying to share here—young children grow so fast, and parents often say: "Oh, my goodness, I wish they wouldn't grow so fast."

This moment, this learning moment, is zooming by for you. On the days where it feels too slow, and there's nothing you can do but lie in your bed because physically you don't feel well, you could, if you like, take this perspective. So you're lying in your bed not feeling well worrying about finances. While you have all that time to lie there and think why don't you reflect on: "I wonder what this lesson is about in my life? Why did I bring in this set of circumstances right now? With the knowledge that I'm going to get out of this, with a lot of grace, but I'm not out of it right in this moment. What is this painful moment showing me about my belief system, my childhood? What's the learning lesson here that's available to me right now?"

In a sense, it is something that is time-limited—like you have often those sales: "you have only 72 hours to buy this at this price!" Well, you have such a short time to learn this lesson before it gets healed or solved and your life moves on. So quick! What is it? What are you learning?

We just want to offer that perspective, because what we have spoken of before still holds true: your main role in this, in terms of getting out of it, is just to become clearer and clearer about what you want. Then when you feel stuck, what you want isn't there yet in a time sense, well, that's because you're in a third-dimensional moment. And you can then take advantage of the learning here. Collectively speaking, you're not going to have so many more moments left of this slower third-dimensional learning. So it's just a different perspective we give about how to enjoy as much as possible the more painful moments here until things move on.

∽

*Q: I feel like from my perspective, the shift has happened. I see some small shifts happening. I'm just wondering how much time to build momentum where I actually feel like I don't have to keep wondering if things that I wish for are going to happen?*

The timing is quite interesting here because you have these two constructs happening at the same moment. So time-bound, let's say, was the old construct. For the most part, you and others are operating as if that still exists. So the construct remains, in a sense, just because people are acting it out. Not because it is a confinement any longer.

And then there is this new construct where time is not there as a limiting factor. So that's where you can get this instant gratification of wishes in ways that don't make sense. Large wishes that should take years but are suddenly there at your doorstep. Because both are in play right now, it's a little bit of an interesting time, and perhaps sometimes a frustrating time, because you taste it, you get that instant reality, but it doesn't work in each case. So why is that?

It is largely because humanity as a whole has not yet woken up to what the new game is. So they're playing by the old rules. That will lessen more and more as people collectively become aware of the change. So how do you approach then, when to know when things are going to happen instantly and when they are not?

It's a little bit of a dance. You can use something which was effective in the past for manifestation, which is to know that it has already occurred. In your own thinking, when you wish for something, if you know that it has already occurred it takes the anxiety out of it. You're not waiting and wondering "if." There is still a question of "when," because so many of the characters in your drama, in your story, here still operating as if time was a constricting factor.

So sometimes it's not instant yet. Not because it can't be, but just because so many people are playing by the old rules. Energetically for you just know as you're wishing for things: "Okay, that's all I have to do. I just wish for it and know that it's already happened." It takes you out of that space of worry about when. "Is this going to be one of the instant ones? Or am I going to wait around wondering if it's going to happen?"

Instead of revisiting those wishes that you hold dear right now, just let them go. Know with great certainty that there are coming true. Don't worry so much about this apparent chaos of wishes that are occasionally happening instantly and occasionally seem to take perhaps not as long as the old way but seem to take time in any case. Understand with compassion that humanity can't quite adapt instantly to this new way of being. And that's the only reason. It's not because there are limits there upon you. But you are in a collective. So even if you could instantly accept your new mastery of this way of being, it would require those around you in the story doing the same thing. So there is likely to be a bit of an adjustment period here for yourself and those around you. And we would say there's no rush.

Isn't it delightful in a way to know that this is what's coming? To know that this is what's available now and to see it play out? When you know it's going to arrive, there's not such a rush to get there. Because it's not a struggle of "if." Is this going to happen in my lifetime? Is it possible? When you remove that question of "if" then time becomes less of a worry.

# THE EASE OF FIFTH DIMENSION

## ANGEL RAPHAEL AND ANGEL ARIEL

*Angel Raphael:*
It is a time of unlimited thinking. Particularly, we are speaking about fifth dimension and what is open there. So you are not misperceiving when you think everything is an option. It is like daydreaming—when you feel that quality, that kind of simple, dreamy quality that doesn't have with it all of that weighty burdened feeling of fears, and the reasons why this is impossible. You're just in that dreamy sort of melting along. That's a good indication that you're there with fifth-dimensional energies and that's the place to "create" from (or to "receive" from is a little more accurate from our perspective). When you're feeling doubt, or: "I think I got this wrong. I don't think that's accessible to me." That's a third-dimensional lens on it.

You're a little more open to receive and move into your more unlimited potentials when you're in that more daydreamy fifth-dimensional state. That's just something for you to recognize, because you'll have both ways of viewing it. It'll go back and forth here for many who are still traveling back and forth between third and fifth quite a lot. When you're in that fifth-dimensional space, and it feels dreamy, almost unreal, that's when you can receive the most—or you can share the most clarity, let's say, without the fears and doubts of what you want moving forward. That's the way to create what you want, to create your own world, is to be in alignment there with dreamy, endless possibilities. There is great truth in that.

∽

*Angel Ariel:*

We want to bring you little bit lighter to close here and bring the energies back into that dreamy fifth-dimensional space. So that if you don't necessarily need to be there right now, we don't need to be talking or viscerally experiencing the third-dimensional slowness, just now. You can dip back into that later if you need to. For now let's come back into fifth and all experience together here what it feels like to be in this remove—slight remove—from our problems and drift—almost this beautiful feeling of drift, and ease, and lightness of the fifth dimension.

You are what you know yourself to be. You have so much freedom to just be what you know, and to know into being.

You don't have to worry about every unconscious thought that goes through your mind. In a conscious sense, what you are focusing on now in these coming years and days is your reality, it is what is going to be shaped for you. So you can have great, great freedom and lightness in knowing that is the case. We're coming out now of the frustration and burden of time into the ease and grace of fifth-dimensional being, which was so effortless.

We are leaving behind what we have learned about how hard, how much time, how much suffering the ways of the world take. That was true then. You weren't misperceiving. But it isn't true in those times now when you're in fifth dimension. You have another delightful delicious realm of experience here for you. Many, many easy, easeful blessings coming your way. And those blessings will be those that you have asked for her. You don't have to worry: "Will they be random? Will they be what I want? Will it be just right for me?" It'll be just what you wish for in that moment. And if you don't like it anymore, you just daydream into something else and change it. You don't have to worry about being locked into some new future. Will it match what you really want?

You are allowed and encouraged to continue to evolve here, as a beautiful being of light, of ease. And you can continue to change your mind and shape the world. Or if you like to think of it this way—rather than changing your mind—if you were sculpting a planet, a new Earth, for yourself you start with the broad brushstrokes. You start with a big lumps of clay, where the continents are. And then you work in those details: "Oh yeah, I really like trees, I want some trees around me." You can start large in your wishing. Or you can start small if you like the details first: "Oh, look at the acorn, how beautiful it is with all those thousands of ridges. Who designed that? It's so beautiful."

It's so easy dears, being in this fifth dimension. And we know you have tasted it already. So know it's going to be more and more of your experience. Less and less will be that frustration of heaviness of time, of struggle, of not knowing how it works, of thinking the only way to get there is through work, through slavery, through money. That was effective before in third dimension. But you're free of all that now. So we encourage you to use third dimension still for learning, when you feel a bit stuck there. And for rest. Sometimes it's a nice place for rest from the higher energies when that feels too much.

Otherwise, to really know that you are going to be drifting more and more in this beautiful, delightful fifth-dimensional space which feels like daydreaming, which feels like love all around you. Which feels like perhaps the reason why people have been trying to chemically alter themselves through drugs and meditation and other means—that kind of delightful, almost altered state of: "Wow, things feel good."

That is what is in front of you dears. And some days you have already tasted this. That is a quality of fifth dimension and is quite sweet, quite wonderful. And quite altered from the perspective of third dimension. It does not feel so concrete or weighty, in that sense. It feels lighter and more removed from such a difficult place as Earth in the third dimension. We invite you to know—whether or not you can believe it or trust it yet—to at least hear this with the ears, with the mind: you're coming into that ease more and more. As angels, our role more and more on this planet is really just to let you know about all of the good news that's around you. And to understand what you're perceiving as things change so much.

# CLOSING PRAYER

## ANGEL URIEL AND ANGEL RAPHAEL

We would like to close with a prayer for those here and for humankind. This is Raphael joined with Uriel.

We wish for you to recognize the magnitude of the moment you are in.

We wish for you to recognize that your heart rules your universe.

We wish for you to recognize that the greatest gift you can give to any other on this planet—whether individually or cosmically as a species—is to reach out with your heart to another and let them know that they are free. We wish for you to create in a space of the heart. No more longing. No more blocks and impediments of the mind to what you truly want. We wish for you to have that full divine love expressed as you wish it in your lifetime.

We wish for you to have a heart beyond measure, connected with the creator's heart. Connected with all that you hold dear. And holding the knowledge in yourself that it is your heart that creates your world as you wish to be.

Above all, we wish you to know that you are free.

We wish you to know that past experience and doubt and what you read in the newspaper is not what guides your world anymore. It is your own heart. So ask your heart what it wants and you are free.

Ask your heart what it wants and you are free.

## ABOUT THE AUTHOR

Adria Wind Horse Estribou is a conscious channel of angels, Lemurians, and other beings who wish to assist humanity.

Adria is a sound shaman, channeling past lifetimes and universal sounds to shift stuck energies. She is also a medium and animal communicator.

She is author of two other books: *Why Did Lemuria Fall?* and *Slip through the Keyhole* and sound healing CD *Sounds of the Ancient Ones*. She is a regular contributor to the *Sedona Journal of Emergence*.

Adria lives in Sedona, and works one-on-one with clients around the world.

At the time of publication, Adria offers live monthly group channeling sessions in Sedona and online, and shares weekly video messages from angels via YouTube and Instagram. You can find out more at www.WingSound.com or @wingsoundhealing.

Made in the USA
Coppell, TX
22 May 2021